FAITHONOMICS

TORKEL BREKKE

Faithonomics

Religion and the Free Market

HURST & COMPANY, LONDON

First published in the United Kingdom in 2016 by
C. Hurst & Co. (Publishers) Ltd.,
41 Great Russell Street, London, WC1B 3PL
© Torkel Brekke, 2016
All rights reserved.
Printed in India

The right of Torkel Brekke to be identified as the author
of this publication is asserted by him in accordance with
the Copyright, Designs and Patents Act, 1988.

A Cataloguing-in-Publication data record for this book is
available from the British Library.

ISBN: 9781849046367 *hardback*

This book is printed using paper from registered sustainable
and managed sources.

www.hurstpublishers.com

For Peter Losonczi (1970–2015)

CONTENTS

CONTENTS

ACKNOWLEDGMENTS

I would like to thank the following people and institutions: the Norwegian Writers Association for financial support; colleagues at the liberal think tank Civita for reading early drafts; Professor Chad Seales of the University of Texas at Austin and Professor Ola Grytten at the Norwegian School of Economics for reading and commenting on an early version of the manuscript; Professor Eva Hamberg of the University of Lund for sharing her knowledge on Swedish religious markets; Dr Shainool Jiwa, head of constituency studies at the Institute of Ismaili Studies (IIS), London, for sharing her knowledge of the government of the Fatimid state and helping with literature on the subject, Dr Ori Goldberg for comments on chapters about Israel, Professor Birgit Weyler and Mr Daniel Pilgrim for help with finding research about German secular rituals, secular-humanist organizations in Norway, Denmark, the UK and Germany for helping me with data about the size of their memberships; and, finally, a large number of colleagues and students at the University of Oslo and the University of Oxford for discussions about religion, politics and economics over many years.

INTRODUCTION

AN ECONOMIC TAKE ON RELIGION

We need to find new ways to think and talk about religion. Public debate about religion is becoming more ill-informed and more divisive every day. In most parts of the world, people have inherited ancient religious traditions that are seen as important providers of public order, morality and a sense of meaning. This is true for Christian, Muslim, Buddhist, Hindu and Jewish societies, and many others. Because of this history, most states support one or several religious organizations. Governments give them subsidies or tax-breaks and have special laws and regulations favoring some religious traditions over others. At the same time, many people are deeply skeptical about the role of religion. Religion is seen as a source of intolerance and violence. Government suppression of religion is increasing and there is wide acceptance of the need to regulate and circumscribe religious life. Relations between governments and religion are fraught with illiberal regulations and practices. There is little separation between religion and the state, and government involvement in religious affairs is on the increase globally.[1]

Americans love to think of their country as the one place on earth where the state keeps a principled distance from religion. But this is pure self-deception as long as religious organizations, and businesses posing as churches, receive billions of dollars in tax-breaks each year. In Europe, we do not even pretend that religions are treated equally, except in France, where they seem to think they have cracked the code of neutrality by imposing a peculiar form of secularism. In Britain, official fear of offending Muslims, Sikhs and Hindus, combined with a taken-for-granted Christian state church, has resulted in what many see as self-defeating multiculturalism.

In the language of economics, the two basic perspectives concerning the roles religion can play can be labeled "public good" and "public bad." One perspective holds that societies need religion because it produces positive things—morality and order—that would disappear if government did not support religion. The other perspective holds that religion creates bad things—like intolerance, gender inequality or terrorism—and therefore governments need to put restrictions on religious life. It is possible, and quite common, for people to hold both perspectives at the same time. They may feel that one or some religious traditions are good and provide society with social glue, while other religious traditions are mere superstitions and create nothing but problems. Which religions you see as good and bad depends on who you are. If you are a Christian, you may see Islam as the problem. If you are a Muslim, you may think the opposite is true. If you are an open-minded Christian or Muslim, you may think that both religions are good, while if you happen to be a hardline atheist, you probably think that both world religions are sources of trouble. Both these perspectives—public good and public bad—lead us astray.

This book offers an alternative. The simple message is that there are markets for religion. There are markets for religious ideas, goods and services and we can see the work of religious organizations, like your local church or mosque, as suppliers of religion. These markets can be more or less free, depending on government regulations and interventions, just like other markets. Economics has developed a set of concepts and theories that is well suited for revealing and explaining the problems that stem from government involvement in the religious market. In Part 3, I examine each of these "deadly sins" of government intervention in religion one by one:

- Crowding Out: The wrong kind of government interference leads to a lack of religious participation and involvement. The process economists call "crowding out" is key to understanding this. Crowding out happens when public funding and support pushes out private donations and participation in the religious sector.
- Rent-seeking: Government interference leads to rent-seeking, which means that an organization spends resources jockeying for privileges and favorable regulations when it sees that government can be influenced. The time and money spent on lobbying amounts to a net loss to society.
- Monopoly: State privileges can lead to a monopoly situation where one very large religious organization dominates the entire market and it is hard or impossible for competitors to get a foothold.
- Discrimination: Lack of the right kind of government regulation often leads to discrimination because powerful religious institutions keep women and gay people, or other groups, out of privileged positions in religious organizations. In economic language, this can be seen as a market failure—a serious and widespread one at that.
- Persecution: There is a link between violence and government intervention in the religious sphere that is mostly overlooked. There is a lively debate among scholars about the causes of terrorism, and recent research shows that the

role played by the state in the religious sphere has a greater effect than we often assume. More importantly, however, there are good reasons to believe that government involvement and favoritism is an important determinant of religious persecution and intolerance in many societies.

- Reification: The zeal of states for ordering, counting and measuring societies is a major cause of the transformation in how people understand religion in the modern world. Religion is reified, which means that it is made into an object in a way it has not been before; the nature of religion has been transformed.

- Imitation: Closely linked to the process of reification is the strong tendency of religious organizations and movements across the world to imitate the type of religion that has been the most successful faith in the twentieth and twenty-first centuries: Protestant Christianity. The sixth and seventh chapters show how religion has become more streamlined and how even atheist organizations have now started mimicking Christian rituals in order to compete in the religious market.

You could be excused for thinking that I have borrowed my title from Steven D. Levitt and Stephen J. Dubner's hugely successful book *Freakonomics* (2005).[2] The subtitle of *Freakonomics* was *A Rogue Economist Explores the Hidden Side of Everything*. However, their idea of everything did not include religion and it would be interesting to know why Levitt and Dubner did not think that religion, too, can be explored with economic concepts and theories. This surely has nothing to do with the relative importance of religion, as it is abundantly clear to most that religion plays a major role in the lives of billions of people. Contemporary media may focus on jihadist terrorism, but there are hundreds of less well-known but fascinating and important cases concerning the political role of religion in people's lives. The *Freakonomics* universe, which now comprises several books and many hours of podcasts and media shows, does not touch on religious organizations and religious phenomena. So if you accuse *Faithonomics* of piggybacking on *Freakonomics*, I would probably answer that my book takes economic thinking into territory that *Freakonomics* should have ventured but never did. I build on the ideas of other authors, of course, but my inspiration mainly comes from a line of literature in economic and sociological theory written by people who are less well known to the general public than the authors of *Freakonomics*.

Karl Marx, the pope and the religious freedom conspiracy

Before I continue, let me say a few words about my point of departure. I grew up in a Communist home in Oslo, Norway. When I was eight, my parents sent me to a guerrilla cell for kids to prepare for the revolution, which would come as an inevitable consequence of deep historical forces, according to Marxist theory. In the language of current political science, I guess I was radicalized. The Communist milieu believed that both the United States and the Soviet Union were evil empires, and they looked at Maoist China as the ideal model for the reinvention of politics and society. The Chinese embassy in Oslo was more than happy to receive us and teach us about the glorious state of affairs in their home country. This was in 1979. The Communist movement in most of Europe was divided along the same lines, between friends of the Soviet Union and friends of China.

I did not particularly enjoy learning Marxist ideology and guerrilla tactics, and I did not see much point in creating a revolution; when I was twelve, I joined a Catholic choir in protest. I was not a Catholic, but I enjoyed singing Mass, listening to the Latin chanting of the priests and smelling the incense. The best thing about it was that we spent many weeks in Rome every summer, where we happened to stand in for the choir in St. Peter's Basilica during their holidays. The great distance between Communism and Catholicism, as well as the similarities in terms of their power over human thought and behavior, was instructive to a child, although it would take some years before I could reflect on these things.

Most of the adults I knew as a child despised religion. They believed, with Marx, that religion had played the role of a smoke screen to cover up the brutality and injustice of the ruling classes, and as false comfort for the downtrodden. They were convinced that religion would vanish once the just Communist society had been established. In the Catholic choir, however, and especially during those long summers in Rome, religion seemed real and important. The beauty and size of St Peter's, the greatest church in the world, witnessed to the power of faith, as did the other magnificent Italian churches in which we performed. Our director interacted with people who belonged to the Vatican establishment, and on special occasions Pope John Paul II (1920–2005) would walk along the rows of boys and touch our heads.

My personal experience of revolutionary Marxism taught me that secular ideologies can function in much the same way as religions. To some people, like my parents, Marxism provided both a worldview (i.e. a comprehensive explanation of human nature and the forces of history) and an ethos (i.e. a collection of norms, rules and motivations for how the world should be). Many have argued that the concept of religion is too historically and culturally linked to Christianity to be of use for comparative and global research. A radical solution to this problem would be to say with the Canadian-born professor of comparative religion, Wilfred Cantwell Smith, that the term religion itself is "confusing, unnecessary, and distorting."[3]

I will not go into the academic controversies over the concept of religion, but I mention this here in order to explain why I am going to include organized atheism in my discussion of religious competition. Anybody interested in the role of religion in the modern world should probably listen to the advice of Ninian Smart, the founding father of religious studies in the UK. He insisted that we need to study religious worldviews alongside secular worldviews such as Marxism, nationalism and organized atheism.[4] When analyzing markets for religion in later chapters, I am going to look at how atheism competes with traditional religion in some Western countries. Looking into the future, this is surely going to be one of the main fault lines in religious competition as various forms of atheisms shape their own systems of belief and ritual and gather believers (or non-believers, as they often prefer to be called) in their own congregations. For my purpose, it would be meaningless to assign atheist organizations and religious organizations to different categories, so in this book the word religion will be used in a very wide sense to include organizations and movements that would not count as religious in a narrow sense.

All scholars of religion will tell you that it is hard, or impossible, to define religion in a satisfactory way. Most will also say that the boundaries between what counts as religion and secular are not stable and change with circumstances. The problem of defining religion brings us to an important reason for writing this book. There is an influential network of scholars in the United States who criticize Western initiatives for international freedom of religion. Their position was formulated in detail in the publications appearing from a research project called "The Politics of Religious Freedom," with its bases at several leading US universities.[5] These academics see initiatives for international religious freedom as deeply misguided, even dangerous. They say that the protection of religious freedom as a universal norm sanctifies a definition or a concept of religion where the individual believer is seen as an autonomous subject who can choose beliefs in a market for religious creeds and organizations. In this view, Western talk about freedom of religion is an attempt to impose the religious marketplace, which they say belongs to the Protestant Christian West, on people in Asia, Africa and Latin America. But this is not all. In the eyes of these academics, the US government's initiatives for international religious freedom are just a cloak to unleash an aggressive brand of American evangelical Christianity, backed by American economic muscle, on the rest of the world.

I agree that the work of some Christian missionary groups is deeply problematic in some parts of the world. The same can be said about some Muslim, Buddhist and Hindu missionary organizations. At the same time, I think that the opinions of the group of scholars I am talking about here are utterly misguided. I am also worried that some of their arguments may play into the hands of the wrong kinds of forces. For dictators who disregard the human rights of minorities, for instance, these ideas effectively provide support to policies based on the claim that religious freedom is impossible because the idea of a religious marketplace is a Western imposition and all talk of religious freedom is an imperialist Christian ploy to proselytize. Hence one reason for writing this book is political. I believe scholars who attack religious freedom initiatives on the grounds they are imperialistic are wrong both in terms of theory and in terms of politics.

PART 1

THE MARKET FOR RELIGION

.

1

SHOULD PRIESTS BE BRIBED INTO LAZINESS?

The market view of religion rests on the work and legacy of the great philosopher and economist Adam Smith, born in 1723 in the Scottish town of Kirkcaldy. Through the publication of his two major works, *The Theory of Moral Sentiments* (1759) and *The Wealth of Nations* (1776), he established himself as one of the greatest philosophers of the Enlightenment, and the founder of modern economic theory. Adam Smith is sometimes caricatured as the man who created the theoretical foundations of an economic system that is destroying the livelihood of common people. Smith's idea of the invisible hand is often taken as a symbol of a cold capitalism that pays no attention to the plight of the poor. This is a misrepresentation of the real and multi-faceted nature of capitalism, and it is certainly a distortion of Smith's thinking. Smith's ideas, although novel and radical in many respects, drew on Christian values of love for one's neighbor with ideas inherited from the classical philosophers of ancient Greece and Rome.

Smith disliked extremes. In order to build his system of moral philosophy, he borrowed ideas about the golden mean described by Aristotle in his *Nicomachean Ethics* and he grappled with the ideas of Plato on several subjects. However,

Smith was even more inspired by the Stoics, a group of philosophers in the ancient world who believed that the wise person must first of all live a virtuous life and exercise right judgment.[1] Excessive consumption or uncontrolled passions are in direct opposition to the Stoic way of life, which values asceticism, reason and tranquility.

A central idea in Smith's thinking is the impartial spectator we all have inside us. This is a consulting judge, he wrote, a "great inmate of the breast," that is able to see our own interests in their proper relation to other people's interests.[2] He saw the virtues of self-control and prudence as essential to leading the right kind of life. Smith is most famous for the idea that self-interest can have good consequences. The idea that self-interest often has consequences that are beneficial for society as a whole goes back to the Stoic philosophers and it is not an idea that is inherently bad or immoral.

An atheist genius

Adam Smith's liberal approach to religion is important to the argument in this book and it is particularly instructive to see Smith's views on the issue in relation to the ideals of his close friend, David Hume (1711–76). Hume, who was probably the greatest philosopher to write in the English language, was extremely interested in, not to say concerned about, the influence of religion on society. Smith first encountered Hume's writings when he studied in Oxford between 1740 and 1746. As a student, Smith was reprimanded for secretly reading Hume's first great work, *Treatise on Human Nature*, in his room; it was considered a heretical book. But Smith and many other students of his generation realized that Hume was the greatest thinker around and they certainly did not stop reading his books and essays because they shocked the religious establishment.[3]

Smith developed a close friendship with Hume between their first meeting in 1749 and Hume's death in 1776. Although Hume was twelve years older than Smith and recognized as a genius, Smith was critical of Hume's almost extreme skepticism. Hume believed that our ability to know the world is limited to the things we can observe and he rejected all kinds of religious speculation. In many of his books, Hume criticized beliefs in miracles or ideas about the nature of God. Many contemporaries saw him as an atheist, which was probably more or less correct.

Two of Hume's books were exclusively about religion. In 1757, he published a book called *The Natural History of Religion*, where he offered his ideas about how different types of religion—like polytheism and monotheism—originated and developed and about the social and political consequences of religion. In the same period, during the 1750s, Hume also wrote a far more critical book called *Dialogues Concerning Natural Religion*. Although this is a difficult and ambiguous text, structured as a dialogue between three people, most readers conclude that its basic argument is that there is no real foundation for belief in God. Hume realized that *Dialogues* was a radical book and he did not dare to publish it. Instead, he let close friends read it. Many of them found Hume far too skeptical and told him so. Hume believed that his thoughts about God were of great importance, and he tried to persuade Adam Smith to take on the responsibility for the publication of *Dialogues* after his death. Hume died in 1776, yet while Smith was extremely fond of Hume, he refused to have anything to do with a book so dangerous.

Arguing the state church

Hume's skeptical view of religion was also evident in his *History of England*, which was published in six volumes between 1754 and 1761. This work was quickly recognized as the best account of England's history. The profits made Hume quite wealthy. Although Smith often rejected Hume's skepticism toward Christianity, one very important idea about the social position of religion in *The Wealth of Nations* can be traced directly to this work. In Chapter 29, Hume discusses the origins of the Reformation, beginning with what he calls a "Digression concerning the ecclesiastical state." The ecclesiastical state is another term for state church. Hume's digression was written, in his own words, to show "why there must be an ecclesiastical order, and a public establishment of religion in every civilized community."[4]

Hume explains that there are two kinds of professions and callings in society. Most of the arts and professions, he writes, are such that they are of benefit both to the individual and to society at large. The simple rule for the magistrate or the government is to leave these arts and professions to themselves and not interfere. The artisans will find that their profits rise if they are able to please their customers and they will increase their skills and adjust their commodities to the demand.[5] But there are also callings and professions that the country needs although no individual benefits from them. These include the civil service and those employed in the army and navy. A government must pay the salaries of these people and attach honors and hierarchies to these professions so that they are attractive.

On the face of it, Hume said, it would seem that the ecclesiastics, the ministers who work for churches and sects, belong to the first category of profession. After all, their "interested diligence" is greatly increased if their subsistence depends on what they get from their flock in exchange for their spiritual ministry and assistance. The reality, however, is that the interested diligence of priests and preachers is exactly what a wise government must prevent. If the priests are too interested in their job, they will go out of their way to attract new followers. Hume used the word "customers" about these followers to indicate how such a situation would work as a market. The best thing that the government can do, Hume wrote, "is to bribe their indolence, by assigning stated salaries to their profession, and rendering it superfluous for them to be farther active ..."[6]

In the *Wealth of Nations*, Book V, Article 3, Adam Smith quoted these passages from Hume's *History of England* in full, referring to his friend as "by far the most illustrious philosopher and historian of the present age."[7] In this part of his work, Smith discussed public expenses and the types of activities that should be paid for by the state. The most obvious example is defense; Smith devoted a lot of space to discussing armies and militias. In Article 3, he discussed institutions for the religious instruction of the people.

Smith's point of departure for his discussion of religion was Hume's distinction between a state church and a free market without public intervention. Smith accepted this distinction, but soon revealed that he did not agree with Hume's conclusions. Whereas Hume believed that a free market for religion would undermine peace and tranquility in society, Smith believed that such zeal would be dangerous only where there is one single sect tolerated by government, or where society is divided into two or three large sects. In a situation with hundreds, or even thousands, of little sects, the zeal of the priests would be altogether innocent, Smith insisted, since no one would be large enough to disturb public peace.

In such a situation, the teachers of each sect, seeing themselves surrounded by adversaries, would be obliged to learn the candor and moderation which one seldom observes among the teachers of great sects that are supported by governments. The teachers of little sects without any public support would be obliged to respect every other sect and this would in time round off their doctrines to a pure and rational religion. Such a plan of no ecclesiastical government has in fact been established in Pennsylvania, where it has resulted in philosophical good temper and moderation, Smith asserted.[8] He concluded his long discussion by saying it would not be unjust if institutions of education and religious instruction were paid by the general contribution of the whole society (i.e. by taxes), but the same expenses could with equal justice, and with advantage, be paid by those who actually use these services.[9]

Free market or state church?

The two philosopher friends disagreed about the ideal relationship between religious organizations and the state. According to Hume, state churches are advantageous to the political establishment if the government can bribe the priests into laziness and inactivity. Hume was a defender of a state church because this system would ensure that the priests were not too interested in their job and were content with providing legitimacy to the powers that be.

In Smith's view, on the other hand, there were greater benefits in a system of no ecclesiastical government, no state church. Smith saw the marriage of one great sect to the dominant political power as dangerous, while the zeal of the ministers of hundreds of little sects would necessarily have to be modified. Smith's idea was that religious diversity would lead to toleration. If only kings and conquerors had never called on the help and support of religious sects and priesthoods, wrote Smith, politics would have dealt equally and impartially with all sects and allowed every man to choose his own priest and his own religion as he thought proper.[10] Smith was convinced that this would have mostly positive consequences for society as no sect would be strong enough to cause trouble and every member of society would be able to shop around for a moral community.

There are many different ways to organize the relationship between religion and the state, but the beliefs and values expressed by Adam Smith and David Hume give us a very good idea of two basic and opposed visions of this relationship. The examples that we can pick from the real world can be placed along a continuum where these two ideals are the end points.

2

BEER, HAIRCUTS AND RELIGIOUS SERVICES

A few years ago, I became a student again. I had been a professor in the study of religion at the University of Oslo for several years. I belong in the field of history and languages, but I have always felt that ignoring the insights from the natural and social sciences is a bad idea, so I decided to enroll in bachelor courses in economics. The University of Oslo has a department of economics that boasts three Nobel Prize winners, so my expectations were high. I was in my mid-thirties. It was exciting to learn something different after spending years immersed in my own field. The basic insight into economic thinking that I received there was crucial for my development as a scholar of religion.

Consuming religion

The economic perspective on religion starts with the same basic concepts as in the traditional areas of economics. Many of the services offered by religious organizations and the people working in them can be analyzed in the same way as products that are sold and bought in markets for goods and services. A religious service in a church, a mosque or synagogue must be produced by somebody. The people behind the production usually have education and training, and they spend time and money in the production process. The building in which the service takes place costs money to buy or rent, and maintain. While planning and preparation may take a lot of time and resources, a religious service is produced in the moment and a religious service cannot be stored for later consumption. This is the case for a range of different consumer services that are sold in markets. For instance, a musical concert or a professional massage for a backache must be produced and consumed at the same time.

A religious service is produced and resources go into its production. But how do people pay for these services? That depends where you look. In many European countries, governments collect taxes from church members. Germany is a good example of the paradoxes and inconsistencies that arise from a historical marriage between religion and state. The religious demography of Germany is a fascinating patchwork. The two dominant religious groups are the Protestant Evangelical Church, which dominates in the northern parts of the country, and the Catholic Church, which is the majority religion in the south and west. The two main churches each have around 23–24 million followers, or roughly 30 per cent of the population. The churches are financed by a church tax (*kirchensteuer*) calculated on the basis of income tax depending on the federal state where one lives. The exact calculations are complex and the system has been undergoing changes in recent years, but in all respects the German church tax is very high. More and more Germans have de-registered to avoid paying tax. Germans are leaving the old Protestant and Catholic churches in hundreds of thousands each year. Yet many of the people who de-register still want to go to church and use its sacraments. In response, the

Catholic Church in Germany issued a decree in 2012 saying that de-registering is a serious lapse and only people who pay their church tax may have a Catholic wedding or burial. So the debates about government taxes for religion have made it obvious to Germans that the services produced are products that must be paid for.

We all accept that butter and flat-screen TVs are produced and sold in a market for consumer goods. Haircuts and other intangible consumer services are the same. But there are things and services where many feel that the logic of the market is misplaced. National defense and street lighting are typical examples. These are public goods. Public goods are goods that would not have been produced, or would have been produced in too small quantities, if they were left to the market because there is no incentive to produce them from the perspective of a market actor motivated by profit. These goods are still important to society and therefore they must be paid for by taxes.

What about religion? Faith is different from butter and haircuts, isn't it? After all, religion is about the really important questions. Whether you are religious or atheist or agnostic, the way you relate to the big questions—is there a God? What happens after death?—is part of your identity, and that of your family and community. Surely, religion cannot be reduced to a commodity? Some critics attack the economic analysis of religion on purely moral grounds, seeing it as an attempt to sneak an evil logic into new areas of human life. Others feel that using economic ideas and language takes away the mystery of the thing we are talking about. But the fact that something is very important to us does not mean that we cannot make rational choices according to ideas about costs and benefits. We do that all the time.

Migration is a good example. There are few things more important than choosing where you want to spend your life and perhaps raise your children. Everybody is born and raised somewhere, and one cannot help feeling a special attachment to one's childhood home. But in the world today, tens of millions of people choose to move to another country each year and many more migrate within large countries like the United States, China or India, often to places that are completely foreign in terms of culture and language. They choose to leave childhood homes and memories, leave family-members and local communities. Some may have a vague idea that they will return in the future, but many never do once they have settled in a new home. Granted, many people move because they are forced to do so by wars and famines. They become refugees. But the number of refugees in a strict political sense is in fact small compared to the masses of people who make the decision to move in search of work.

In the summer of 2013, I made the choice to migrate when I moved from my home in Oslo, Norway, to a job in the Faculty of Theology in the University of Oxford. I know something about the hours and days one spends calculating costs and benefits. I am not only talking about costs and benefits in terms of salaries and relocation expenses. On the contrary, perhaps the most important calculations were about my relationship to friends and family-members and about the relative importance of being part of the culture and society in which I was raised. A year later, I returned to Norway because my family did not want to move and was tired of flying from Norway to the UK every week.

So the fact that religion is really important to many people is not an argument against seeing religious behavior as subject to calculations of costs and benefits. It is reasonable to say that people's use of religious services, their participation in worship and rituals, and their interaction with religious leaders—priests, rabbis, imams, monks—are elements of behavior that is rational. This does not mean that the behavior is the result of a cynical calculation of profit maximization. A serious analysis of behavior must take into account that choices made by individuals are restricted by the available information and their ability to use it. People are guided by their personal preferences and tastes, they are restricted by the rules and norms of social institutions and they are subject to a number of other constraints.

How do you spend your Sunday?

Imagine two people—John and Jane—who both wake up one Sunday morning in the same town. John gets up and drives to church where he stays for an hour and gives 10 dollars in alms. Jane looks at her watch, turns around and sleeps another thirty minutes. Then she gets up and goes running for thirty minutes before she starts making breakfast. Is it possible to use economic ideas to analyze their behavior? Clearly, John is giving up several things to use the service offered by his local church. He spends his time and money, necessarily forfeiting other uses of those resources. To Jane, the time and money that go into visiting church does not seem to be worth it.

Several other things could be part of the explanation why John chooses to spend his resources on religion while Jane chooses differently. Perhaps Jane's car is broken so it is difficult for her to get to church. Perhaps John has recently experienced a life-crisis, which makes it more attractive for him to go to church on this particular day. The complex totality of reasons can only really be grasped if we get inside both of their heads—as outside observers, we can only be certain that one of them spends time and money on religion this Sunday and the other one does not.

We can devise clever questionnaires measuring beliefs and tastes, but in the end we cannot get inside other people's heads. For a sociological or economic analysis, the most important elements in religion are not belief and faith, but the collective and public aspects of religion. These are things we can see and measure. We can count how many times John and Jane go to church every year and this would be one way to gauge their demand for religion. We could do the same on a bigger scale by counting the total number of church visits in their town per year relative to the number of inhabitants. This would give us a crude measure of the demand for religion in the local community. Another way would be to look at the amount of money John and Jane donate in alms to their local churches each year, or the total sum given in alms to all the churches in their town.

Defining religious markets

Even though it is clearly the case that religious services have to be produced by somebody and that users actually pay for them in some way or another, I suspect that many readers will intuitively say that religion is something completely different from the goods and services we buy and sell in markets. But what is a market? Economists have different approaches to pinning down the meaning of this contested concept. Some claim that "in the beginning there were markets" and insist that markets arise naturally and spontaneously wherever people interact. Some tie the concept of market to a place, the marketplace, where voluntary exchange goes on. Others see the concept of market as detached from locality—after all, exchange takes place over vast distances and by ever new technological channels, and elements in the transaction can take place at different times. Economists will never find the perfect definition of the word "market," but they roughly know what they mean by it. On the most general level, the key element of any market is voluntary exchange between parties. The parties in the markets are sellers and buyers. When they meet, their supply and demand establishes prices.

In the most concrete sense, then, a religious market is the mechanism or means by which religious goods are exchanged. The market in which religious goods are exchanged is a market with unclear boundaries. Very often, it is important to look closely at the secular environment in order to understand the behavior of a church or a mosque or a temple.[1] New government restrictions, new laws or changes in taxes and subsidies, can amount to changes in the environment of a religious organization that lead to changes in behavior. A Christian congregation may feel more threatened by a new shopping mall than by a neighboring Christian church or a Hindu temple. Some of the examples I will use in a later chapter are about the challenge to traditional Christian monopolies from atheist organizations in the market for rites of passage in parts of Europe.

It is possible to get a clear idea of what is being exchanged in religion and it is possible to get a clear picture of the basic parties doing the exchange. Nevertheless, many will object to all this by saying that it is easy to define "normal" markets (for TVs, for beer, for haircuts) and difficult to define a market for the religious goods discussed here. This is not true.

Defining a religious market in history or today is no more or less difficult than defining other types of markets. Let us take an example from the world of business. In the United States, the set of rules and laws established to make sure there is sufficient competition in the market is called "anti-trust law," and in the EU it is called "competition law." Under these jurisdictions, several kinds of business practices or operations are unlawful because they restrict competition, for instance by concentrating too much market-power in the hands of one firm. This can result in one firm getting a monopoly (I will return to the problem of religious monopolies in a later chapter). For the sake of comparison, take a simple product like beer. If two large producers of beer wanted to merge, it could be the case that the new, larger firm would control such a large percentage of the beer market that there would be little competition left. Or if a large producer of beer decided to cut the price of its beer below its own cost in making the beer simply in order to undermine the business of smaller competitors, then this could be a case of what economists and lawyers call predatory pricing, which is unlawful.

One of the fundamental problems in legal cases concerning competition law involves defining the market for some good or service. In the case of beer, how big is the market? Is a country like India, the United States, Germany or the UK one market? Or a specific region of that country? What about the EU as a whole? What is to be included in the relevant market? Ale? Stout? Wine? Soft drinks? Cider? Alcopops? The two parties in a legal case over market dominance will often disagree in the most fundamental ways on how to define "the market." The range of cases concerning competition law demonstrates that even seemingly simple markets like "the beer market" can be hard to delimit and pin down for practical purposes.[2] So, the difficulties we may or may not have with identifying and delimiting religious markets makes them no different from other markets. The unclear boundaries of the religious markets are not something that make this market radically different from the beer market.

Supply and demand

Do people always have a need or craving for religion? Is demand more or less constant? This is a contentious issue for sociologists of religion. For several decades, the prevailing belief among scholars was that religious demand was steadily on the decline and in the long term this would result in religion becoming extinct. A fundamental reason for the decline in demand, according to this view, was that religion traditionally provided safety and security in a dangerous world. In the modern period, said the theory, we have the medicines, the technologies and the affluence to keep us safe, so we no longer need religion. Religion was becoming superfluous and demand would dwindle. This was the secularization hypothesis, which ruled during the 1960s and 70s.

The economic theory of religion was a challenge to the theory of secularization. In fact, it was already clear in the 1990s that scholars of religion were fighting a battle over two opposing theoretical models of how to understand religion in the modern world. Proponents of the economic theory believe that demand for religion is constant over time, while proponents of secularization theory believe that religious demand was high in the past and has declined steadily over the past three centuries. Secularization theory sees a steady decline, while economic theory attacks the idea that history was more religious than the present and the future, debunking the myth of past piety.[3]

According to market theory, a wide and diverse supply of religious options will lead to more religious consumption, more participation in religious services. Supporters of secularization theory have regularly claimed the exact opposite, saying that diversity undermines the credibility of any particular religion, causing religious decline. The problem with these opposing claims is that demand for religion is very difficult to measure. One can measure actual consumption of religion by counting the number of times people participate in religious worship or by counting how much time and money they spend on religion. But there can be circumstances under which real consumption is low, as in Communist or other repressive societies, and then it becomes almost impossible to say anything about the latent demand for religion in society.

It is easier to measure the supply-side of the religious market. We can count the number of churches, sects and denominations in an area and their relative sizes, we can count the number of priests, imams, rabbis or monks in a town or community and we can count the total number of religious services given in the area. The supply-side of religion is determined by the groups and organizations offering religious services. If there is a great number and diversity of such organizations, chances are that there is a wide choice of options and hence a good supply of religion. In other words, the supply of religion is about the degree of diversity among the organizations and people offering services. It is about the availability of choice.

Imagine two different countries, both with ten different religious organizations. We can call them the United States and Sweden, bearing in mind that this is just a thought experiment. Let us assume that ten religious organizations in the United States have 10 per cent of the market each, while in Sweden one church has 90 per cent of the market, and ten other groups have 1 per cent each. The two countries have the same number of religious organizations, but religious diversity in the United States is much higher than in Sweden. We can draw a parallel to other goods and services. A country where one huge producer supplies 90 per cent of the bread is less diverse than a place where ten roughly equal bakeries supply 10 per cent each. The same for haircuts. The supply-side in bread and haircuts is better with many small suppliers because they would adjust to consumer demand by competing in quality and price, and by exploring niches in the market.

The religious market goes online

Just before Christmas 1998 my wife and I boarded a plane to San Francisco and spent a month staying with friends. My wife had just finished her degree in clinical psychology at the University of Oslo and I had just handed in my doctoral thesis in Oriental Studies at the University of Oxford. We were in our late twenties and had a baby boy drooling in his seat as we drove around and marveled at the glass-buildings of Silicon Valley and talked to people our age who were working in exciting tech companies. It was obvious that something was changing in a profound way, and when we got back to Oslo, we decided to borrow some money from a bank and set up what was probably Europe's first online psychological counseling service. My wife spent many hours by the keyboard counseling on various issues, but after half a year she was forced to shut down because the company that hosted the website was not able to provide the online security that met the very rigorous standards of the authorities.

The internet is transforming the way we live our lives, not least the way we buy and sell things. Is it changing the religious marketplace, too? Undoubtedly. A few of the early studies argued that social interaction is not a significant part of life online and this would make it impossible for religion to thrive in cyberspace.[4] Religion is, after all, something with a fundamental social element to it. Religion, in order to be religion, requires not only a set of ideas and values that are shared by a group of people. It also requires some sort of communal experience. The emotions that arise when people come together and pray, sing and perform rituals are a fundamental element of religion in prehistory and today. If we sit alone in front of our screens and discuss philosophical ideas with individuals on the other side of the world it does not qualify for the label "religion," even if the ideas we discuss are about life after death or the nature of God. For a start, we often have no way of verifying the true identity of the people we communicate with on the web if we have not interacted with them offline. Some people change identities or use nicknames. It makes little sense to say that you belong to a religious group if you cannot be sure that other members really are who they say they are. Do you feel you really share an experience with somebody who calls himself Linda one day and Buffy the Vampire Slayer the next? Religion must have some communal aspect to it and internet technology does not seem to offer that kind of experience.

This may be part of the reason why we have not seen any successful and long-lasting cyber-religions, in the sense of religious groups that arise and exist only on the internet. In fact, one of the main findings of research about religion and the internet is this: religion online is mostly an extension of religion offline. Traditional religious groups use the internet in the same ways as other organizations, as when the pope tweets about Christ and forgiveness as @Pontifex and the Dalai Lama about compassion or anger management as @DalaiLama. Traditional religious organizations and leaders use the web to disseminate information about their activities, to explain doctrine, post material, sometimes to offer counseling.

But this does not mean that everything is business as usual. Traditional religions are affected and challenged by internet technology in several ways. The building up of individual religious identities is more flexible and more fragmented than is usually the case in offline religion. This flexibility and fragmentation creates new freedoms because individuals can shop around for the resources to build a religious identity. So the internet can empower people, but for the same reasons it is a great challenge to traditional sources of religious authority. The same is true for many other sectors and markets. The internet empowers individuals and challenges old structures of authority. The internet allows people without any proper training or credentials to rise to the role of instant experts through their skills in maneuvering and arguing in virtual reality. Often, religion online challenges both the doctrinal contents and the hierarchies of traditional religion.[5] But these developments are taking place in religion offline as well. In the offline world, religious authorities are being challenged in various ways. The individualization, fragmentation and idiosyncrasy of online religion must be seen in relation to parallel trends in offline religion. Most believers try to connect their lives offline and online; values and beliefs floated online are seldom radically removed from offline realities.

So authority structures are crumbling partly because of the internet. This is nothing new in the history of religions. Many commentators have compared the effects of the internet on religious authority to the effects of printing technology in the Reformation. Martin Luther and other reformers of the 1500s would never have reached such a spectacularly large audience if their religious protest movements had not coincided with the invention of the printing press. When I teach a course on religion and politics, I like to show my students photos of two items from the interior of Luther's house in Wittenberg: a printing press and a sword. Religious change needs political power, a sword to back it up, and it needs the right technology to reach an audience; 500 years ago it was printing, today it is the internet.

Almost all of the research about religion online has been about "Western" religions. (I put Western in quote marks because ideas of west and east are slightly out of place in virtual reality and also because Christianity will soon have more offline members in the south and east than in the west.) In the world of Hinduism, for example, the internet is starting to become a threat to authority in some places. There are now websites where Hindus around the world can order and pay for devotional rituals to be performed at the Kalighat temple in Kolkata. This undermines the authority of the professional priests attached to the temple.[6] The same seems to be happening in several other important Hindu temples across India.

The novel element in this trend is not the buying and selling of religious services. As I show in the historical parts of this book, such buying and selling has taken place throughout history. In the world of pre-Hindu, Vedic India, 3,000 years ago, wealthy people would pay religious specialists,

Brahmins, to carry out rituals on their behalf and the relationship between the sponsor of the sacrifice and the sacrificer was crucial to the early development of Indian religion. Today, an Indian middle-class family in London or New York can order similar sacrifices on the internet to be carried out for them in India. What is radically new here is not the payment and the exchange of services, but the distance, the choice available to the consumer, and the ease of the transaction. The market for the rituals simply works more smoothly: after the sacrifice is finished, the consumer receives a neat package with the leftovers of the food or other substances offered to the god. Distance may alter the experience of the sacrificial ritual, but in the worldview of the people using these online services the efficacy of the ritual is the important thing.

So the internet clearly has consequences for how established religions go about their daily business and this is true for all the world religions. But so far all attempts to establish religions online without any offline presence have been short lived and unsuccessful. This might change and I am tempted to believe it will change sooner rather than later. Technology develops at ever increasing speed. My wife's counseling service would be easy to set up now, seventeen years after her pioneering attempt; there are many of these services online today. In a short time from now we may see technology that enables rich communal experiences in cyberspace. We can think of helmets and goggles to provide senses of vision, sound and smell, or body-suits that produce different sensations.

The world of online games gives a hint of the future of cyber-religion. World of Warcraft (WoW) is currently the most successful of the Massive Multiplayer Online Role-Playing Games (MMORPG) with well over 10 million subscribers, far more than any other online game. In the WoW universe, a great variety of religious activity takes place. Players can choose to be shamans, druids or priests, among many other things. The WoW universe is full of "real" religion as well. For example, the game developers at Blizzard (the company that makes WoW) have created numerous memorials inside the game to honor deceased loved ones— that is, real people, not game characters. Such memorials come in many shapes, often as straightforward tombstones and graves with a poem or verse to the dead person, but they also come in the form of quests and narratives that are meant to retrace and memorialize periods or events in the lives of a deceased friend or family member.[7]

The religion that is popular in the gaming world is typically inspired by non-Abrahamic traditions, like Buddhism, Hinduism, shamanism or more diffuse spiritual practices. Many of the biggest online games are teeming with spirits, gods and goddesses, and characters are constantly engaged in activities or groups that would typically be classified as "alternative religions" or "cults" if they took place offline. The global gaming communities are often countercultural in their rejection of Christianity, and Christian activists have realized the danger to Christianity online and launched responses. Conflicts over religion are as fierce online as they are offline, and most of the time conflicts online are extensions of conflicts offline.

What happens to the religious marketplace when religion goes online? To answer this, we need to ask what happens to markets in general when they move to the internet. They become smoother, they connect consumers with suppliers in far more efficient ways, they give unprecedented freedom of choice, they reduce the prices of things that used to be expensive and break up old monopolies. There is no reason to think that religious markets will behave in radically different ways. Does this mean that religious consumption will increase online? That could be. We do not know yet, but to expect religion to disappear because of internet technology is like expecting people to stop listening to music because Napster, Spotify and Wimp are offering us all the music we want online.

3

PRIESTS AND FIGHTER PILOTS

Do you think that people are basically good or basically bad? If you woke up tomorrow and found that your country no longer had a government, do you think that people in your neighborhood would start to cooperate and exchange things for their mutual benefit? Or do you think they would kill each other and steal each other's stuff to secure their own livelihood? The proper scope of government has always been the main topic of discussion for political theorists. Writers who believe that people are basically good, like the great English philosopher John Locke, think that government should limit itself to upholding basic rights and refrain from interfering in people's lives, while those who think we are basically bad, like the equally great English philosopher Thomas Hobbes, think that government must be big and strong to restrain the killer inside us.

Adam Smith claimed that governments have three roles to fulfill. First, they must provide national defense. Secondly, they must establish civil justice. Finally, governments must provide those public institutions and public works that are advantageous to society but of such a nature that the profits could never repay the expenses to an individual or a small number of individuals.[1] Institutions and works that are of value to society as a whole but unprofitable to private entrepreneurs must be created and maintained by the state. Adam Smith's analysis of public goods was not very sophisticated, however, and his examples are actually misleading. He writes about roads, bridges and canals as public goods, but the fact is that such works have often been funded by private money. This is beside the point. The crucial question concerning faulty policies regarding religion is this: does religion belong to the class of public institutions or public works that are advantageous to society but unprofitable to the individual?

Do religious groups produce public goods?

Think about the armed forces protecting your country from invasion and intimidation by other states. Whether you are a hardline militarist or a pacifist, you know that building up and maintaining the armed forces is one of the most expensive ventures in which human societies engage. In modern times, the cost of war has grown exponentially for the simple reason that technology is so expensive, and in military affairs, when the going gets tough, having the technological edge is everything. A modern fighter jet can cost US$100 million per plane and we need to add to that an enormous amount of infrastructure and training.

The good provided by an air force is national security. Every person living in a country enjoys this security. I do not ponder these things every day, but when dramatic events take place on the international stage, like the conflict over Ukraine or the warlike rhetoric between Iran and Israel in recent years, thoughts about national security sometimes cross my mind. Security is not always a public good. Think of private security companies, or even mafias, that provide protection against payment. National security is different for a couple of very important reasons. The consumption of national security by one person causes no subtraction from any other individual's consumption. My enjoyment and use of national security does not diminish yours. National security is a non-rival good.

In addition, it is impossible for national security to exclude particular persons or groups. Imagine that the armed forces started a subscription system where all citizens could decide whether they would be part of a national security scheme by paying a monthly bill. Your neighbor pays up, but you decide the subscription is too expensive. Bad luck: your country is invaded by foreign troops and the armed forces only protect the houses, gardens and apple trees of the people who were smart enough to subscribe to national protection. Such a system of payment would not work because national security is by its nature non-excludable.

The basic problem with private payment for public goods is that we would all have strong incentives to lie about our demand for these goods. I know perfectly well that the armed forces cannot avoid protecting me as well as my neighbor in case of war, so if they ask me to subscribe to their services, I will simply say I do not think I need them, thank you. I will free ride and nobody can stop me. Therefore, there is clearly no way that building up a modern air force would make economic sense for a private entrepreneur. Without a government to make decisions about public expenditure on national security we simply would not have it.

The same argument is made about religion in several countries. The goods and services national religions provide are non-rival and non-excludable. If I go to church in, say, the UK or in Denmark, my consumption of religion does not diminish the amount of religion that others can consume and it is not possible to exclude me from these goods either. When my Muslim friends go to their mosque, or my Jewish friends to the synagogue, or my Hindu friends to their temple, their consumption is just as non-rival and non-excludable as my use of a church. On the face of it, then, religion seems to be a public good in many countries.

Religious organizations sometimes contribute to the social, moral and cultural life of a nation. Mind you, I have not said anything about whether this contribution is positive or negative. In fact, I think that kind of discussion is not very interesting because it is impossible to solve. Angry atheists insist that religion has negative effects. I am not prepared to engage in that argument, although I do find that their historical and sociological understanding of religion is sometimes limited. Conservative believers think that societies, or even individuals, without religion are less moral and more prone to violence and theft. That is nonsense. Do psychologists and sociologists test these questions? Yes. Are their results interesting? Not really. The research questions too often seem to be guided by personal convictions and prejudice. We do not need to agree on the question of whether religion has a mostly positive or negative effect on society. People may disagree over whether the armed forces have a positive or negative role to play in human societies, but this argument has no bearing on the question of whether national security should be analyzed as a public good.

For the sake of argument, let us follow the logic of those who claim that a national religion produces public goods, like social cohesion or social integration arising from a shared identity or sense of community, or a moral order arising from a shared commitment to the moral standards of the group or from fear of God. If a national religion provides public goods in this sense, if it can reasonably be compared to national defense, the logical extension of our thinking would be to say that there is no way to determine the actual demand for religion, because of problems like free-riding. I would simply not pay for membership in a church as long as I know that I cannot be shut out from its services. From this perspective, it seems the government needs to make the decisions about public spending on religion, just as it does with regard to fighter jets and lighthouses. It would collect taxes, that is what governments do, and through democratic voting, we (the people) would tell the democratic system roughly how much we think a government should spend on public works like national security or national religion.

The problem with national religion

From our discussion so far it seems we have determined that religion is a public good like national defense. We have followed the political logic of many of the countries that have state religions. The only problem is that we have built the discussion on a conceptual flaw. When discussing armed forces as a public good we easily lose sight of the fact that armies were first raised not to protect a collective, not to shield a nation against other nations, but simply to secure the interests of kings and barons. The security provided by the armies of medieval times was like the services provided by security companies or mafias. Soldiers and equipment were paid for by wealthy private individuals, and the security produced was enjoyed by the same individuals and their families and friends. There was no national security because there were no nations.

The institutions we think of as national religions or national churches were also established for reasons completely different from the welfare of nations. In Protestant Europe, national churches were the creation of kings who wanted to wrest power from the Holy Roman emperor and confiscate the immense riches of the Catholic Church. The Protestant kings ruling northern Europe from the mid-1500s set themselves up as heads of national churches. They crushed the old power structure of the Catholic bishops and made the churches obey secular power.

These were not national churches in our sense. They were state churches established and ruled by powerful monarchs. Religion was subject to intense control both in the Catholic lands in southern Europe and in the new Protestant states. People were forced to pay church taxes and to attend services. Responsibility was private. If you broke the laws or did not pay your share, you could be excluded from participating in your local church. In other words, religion did not come close to being a public good. Exclusion was serious. It meant you did not have access to the really important things in life—or in death. The church delivered all the life-cycle rituals—baptism, confirmation, wedding, burials—and without good standing in your church you did not have access to the ultimate religious good: salvation.

There is no sense in talking about national defense or national religions before there are nations. So when did nations enter the limelight of history? Some historians say that the roots of nations should be traced back to the fifteenth or sixteenth centuries, but most believe they came into existence more recently, perhaps only after the French Revolution. I do not think that we will ever get a unanimous verdict from the camp of professional historians about the question of how old nations and national consciousness really are because the sources they use to answer the question can be read in very different ways.

We can be sure, however, that national churches that deliver goods and services that are non-rival, non-excludable and entirely publicly funded did not appear before the nineteenth century. This was a period when new communication technologies made national consciousness much easier to mediate to the masses and it was the period when politics was often about how to build inclusive and healthy nations. Both militaries and churches were key to early state building from the 1500s, but only from the 1800s did they become elements in forging nations.

Classifying religious goods

To determine whether religious organizations produce public goods or not, we have to go deeper into the different types of goods and services they supply. Across cultures and through history, religious groups have provided a wide range of very different goods and services. Let us start by classifying these according to two criteria. We ask whether the products offered by religious organizations are rival or non-rival, and whether they are excludable or non-excludable. This gives the simple table in Figure 1 (overleaf).

Some of the sociological and economic literature about religion argues that the primary good religion offers is salvation and that religion is first and foremost a relationship of exchange between human beings and supernatural beings. Humans are afraid to die, they are fundamentally and understandably uncertain about what will happen after death and they are often willing to pay to get some kind of assurance from a divine being about their ultimate fate. This is the basis for the theoretical work by Rodney Stark, who has made some of the most important contributions to the economic theory about religion.

Figure 1: Classification of religious goods

	Excludable	*Partly excludable*	*Non-excludable*
Rival	Rites of passage Individual absolution	*Congested* worship services, social events, public lecture	
Non-Rival	Salvation Collective absolution	*Uncongested* worship services, social events, public lecture	Prayer calls, church bells Social cohesion? Social integration? Moral order?

I certainly agree that salvation is an essential product offered by many of the major religions. This is the case with the systems we have come to label "world religions" in modern times, in particular Christianity, Islam and Buddhism. On the other hand, there are plenty of religious systems that are not very interested in salvation. If we look for ideas of salvation in the religion of Australian Aborigines, or the Lapps of northern Sweden, we do not get very far, or we run the danger of distorting our data. More importantly, many people who belong to religions are more interested in other elements in their religious tradition than what happens in the afterlife. For some people, the relevance of salvation is also a question of timing. When you are twenty-five you may want to use the services of your church or mosque or synagogue to get married, but your hormones keep you preoccupied by things other than death. If you reach ninety and feel weak and ill, ideas about the afterlife may seem more relevant.

Different types of religious goods must be classified differently. In most religious systems, salvation is a non-rival good. Although some traditions teach that only a specific number of people can be saved and the rest are doomed, the most common conception of salvation assumes that the amount of salvation available will not be diminished by people getting it. If all my neighbors and colleagues go to hell, that does not increase my chances of being saved.

However, salvation has mostly been an excludable good. There is an enormous number of conceptions of salvation, but in the world religions it has been possible to exclude individuals from salvation on account of what they have or have not done, or because they fail to pay the religious organization and its specialists who deal in salvation goods. The guardians of salvation in Christianity are the priests, although they have lost this role in many modern societies. In the medieval church, considerable creativity went into designing new products concerned with salvation, like the late medieval sale of indulgences, by which an individual could be spared the punishment of sins in purgatory.

Some systems of religion are highly individualized and have conceptions of salvation in which the mediating role of a religious organization is no longer needed. This is typical of some of the new religions that reject all kinds of hierarchy and insist on the individual's direct relationship with the divine or transcendent reality. The type of salvation envisaged by such systems, however, is not interesting from an economic point of view because there is no exchange, no transaction and no production process that is taken care of by a religious organization, publicly funded or not.

Many of the most important products on offer by religions are both rival and excludable. Take rites of passage. It takes a religious specialist a lot of work to plan and perform the necessary actions required for a name-giving ceremony, a wedding or a burial. The more I consume of these goods the less time and resources the religious organization will have for other people's rites of passage. It is possible for a religious organization to say to me that I cannot baptize my daughter or bury my grandfather if I do not pay.

In most religious traditions there is a range of other religious goods in which an individual interacts with a specialist or an organization to get help or advice. For example, Christian churches have institutionalized forgiveness for sins in a rite called absolution. The ritual surrounding absolution mostly involves some kind of confession of sins and a priest's forgiveness. The different branches of Christianity diverge over whether absolution is mostly a private or a collective rite. When absolution is given collectively to a congregation in church it is a non-rival good, but when it is given individually by a priest after confession, it is clearly a rival good.

There are virtually no religious goods I can think of that by their nature are non-rival and non-excludable, but to make the case we could perhaps think of very public displays of religion, like the chiming of church bells or Islamic prayer calls, as religious goods. The conclusion is that most religious goods are by nature either what economists call private goods, because they are both rival and excludable, or club goods because they are non-rival and excludable. Religion hardly offers goods that are by their nature public goods.

Why, then, has the political regulation of religion in most modern states been based on the misguided idea that religious goods are public and should be funded by governments? I will try to answer that question in the next chapter, but first we should take a look at a kind of religious good that falls between the purely private and public.

Religious organizations as clubs

Many of the most important goods produced by religious groups are private goods, and it is unlikely that religions are important in the production of pure public goods. However, private and public goods are not the only type of goods that are relevant to the discussion of the religious market. Religious groups can often be analyzed as clubs, which means they are societies where the members work together to produce a class of goods called club goods. The characteristic features of club goods place them somewhere between purely private and purely public goods. Club goods are excludable, like private goods, but exclusion is often costly and impractical. In Figure 1, I have placed them in a column as partly excludable to keep them apart from purely private and purely public goods. Club goods are also non-rival, like pure public goods, as long as the number of people using the good does not get too high. When a club has too many members, when too many people use its premises or services, it starts becoming crowded. A typical example is a park, which is normally a public good where there is no rivalry in consumption. Yet if thousands of people flock to the park on a sunny day during the holidays, things start to look different. At that point, the park as a public good has become congested and it is better seen as a club good rather than a public good. The problem of congestion means that the size of membership is important for organizations offering typical club goods.[2]

Think of the goods produced by a football club for kids. I was never a good football coach. As the academic type I lacked the natural authority and self-assuredness that you need in order to shout clear instructions to ten- or twelve-year-old boys from the sideline. I have a loud voice, but I also had a habit of undermining my own words by adding "maybe" or "if you feel you are up to it today." But then again my children never were any good at football and soon switched to things like horse-riding from which I am excluded by allergy. Still, I want to believe it was better for my children and their friends to have me than to have no football coach at all. I was investing a considerable amount of time and energy in producing a good that was consumed freely by any child in our neighborhood who wanted to take part. A great number of people actually contribute in this way to club goods by giving away their own private money or spending their time and energy on collective projects.

Examples of club goods produced by religious groups include worship services, public lectures or a social gathering. All these activities share the features of pure public goods up to a certain point. A service in a church or a mosque or a synagogue or a temple can be enjoyed and shared by anybody without diminishing the experience of anyone. In Figure 1, I have placed these activities as rival or non-rival depending on the degree of congestion. In fact, the quality of these goods increases with the participation of new and enthusiastic participants because some of the religious experiences are fundamentally collective and require input from a group.

That is why the quality and intensity of the members' participation is an important focus for the club model when applied to religious groups. A club ideally produces a good experience for every member, but this requires that many of the members really invest money, time, energy and enthusiasm in the activities of the club. If you have been to a Pentecostal service somewhere in the world, you know what this means. The experience is intense because the people present are often animated and emotional. In a Pentecostal or Charismatic service, people use their voices and their bodies to create a total religious experience. This is the level of enthusiasm and commitment that clubs are after because this is what creates the quality of the club good that is produced. The problem is that a club that can offer this kind of experience is open to new members who lack the requisite enthusiasm and commitment. They want the experience without investing all the time, money and energy in the club that other members put in. In other words, they are free-riders.

Free-riding

The problem of free-riding is not always easy for religious clubs to overcome. The congregation may ask for donations and it may want members to attend services regularly, but it can hardly monitor enthusiasm and commitment, it cannot measure the loudness of the singing or the authenticity of its members' emotional expressions. Laurence R. Iannaccone has suggested that this problem is the reason why many sects demand so many seemingly irrational sacrifices from their members.[3] It seems to be a universal trait of sects that they tell members to behave in certain ways or observe certain rules that involve a sacrifice. Sometimes such behaviors and rules can even stigmatize the member in the eyes of the outside society, as when people dress in unfamiliar clothes, or chant "Hare Krishna" in the street. Such behaviors, Iannaccone suggested, are rational ways for religious clubs to screen out potential members who lack the commitment and enthusiasm needed to be of value to the congregation in the continued production of a religious experience. The commitment of members of strict sects can also be seen in monetary terms. In the United States, members of sects tend to give more money in charitable giving than others despite the fact that they generally have a lower income and lower levels of education, factors that are generally associated with less charitable giving.[4]

Because club goods are sensitive to the number of people using them, clubs need to think about their size. Research applying a club model to Christian congregations in the United States suggests that congregations should look for an optimal size in terms of members if they want to maximize the commitment and generosity of the congregation. This is because each new member in a religious group increases the benefits to the club in at least two ways: a new member means that fixed costs to the congregation can be spread over a higher number of participants, and it means that the experience of fellowship and community might increase for all members. After the club has reached its optimal size, however, new members diminish the total experience because of crowding. But in addition to the problem of crowding, the continued success and growth of a sect is a threat in another more important way. It will start attracting people who are less inclined to make investments in the group's communal life in terms of money and time. While they want to experience the good things the religious club produces, they do not want to contribute their fair share: they are free-riders. This means that growth and success is good, but only up to a certain point because after that the negative effects will outweigh the benefits.[5]

This chapter was intended to clear up the widespread misunderstanding that religion provides pure public goods in the shape of social cohesion, social integration or moral order. Take a quick look at Figure 1 again: the work of religious organizations and the goods they produce are private goods, mainly in the shape of rites of passage, including rituals surrounding birth and name-giving, rituals concerning the transition from adolescent to adult, wedding rituals and burials. In addition, many of the goods produced by religion are club goods that are partly excludable and non-rival up to the point where congestion sets in. The goods in the bottom right corner of Figure 1, goods that are really non-excludable and non-rival, are negligible and should not take our attention away from the aspects of religious life that are important. However, to convince you that this really is a misunderstanding, we need to look into where the idea of religion providing public goods comes from in the first place. That is the subject of the next chapter.

4

FAITH AS SOCIAL GLUE

THE HISTORY OF A BAD IDEA

Over the past couple of decades, new debates have emerged about the role religion plays in society. Many of the debates take as their basic assumption that religion can have two straightforward roles. It can create social cohesion and harmony, or it can create hostility and violence. The question then becomes how government can best nurture the good religion and limit the bad. But the question is misguided.

Tax-breaks—or how to be religious about rug-cleaning

In most countries, tax authorities treat certain kinds of non-profit organizations in fundamentally different ways from normal profit-seeking firms because government and society see non-profits as fulfilling some kind of public good. These are, for example, charitable, educational or religious organizations. Normally, national tax-collecting agencies have the right to determine whether an organization fulfills the criteria for tax-exemption. It is extremely common, for instance, for the donations given by private individuals to religious organizations to be deducted from the individual's income tax. In Western countries like the UK, Germany and the United States, tax-exemptions amount to very substantial sums of money as corporate tax, income tax and different types of property and sales taxes do not apply, or apply only partly, to religious organizations. The logic behind tax-exemption for religious organization is that they belong to a class of organizations that serve the public, they are of benefit to the community and society at large, and do not serve private interests. The assumption that religion provides public goods and should therefore be exempt from tax is made explicit in the laws of many countries or in court cases where laws are applied. In other words, tax laws tell us a lot about how people, societies and governments think about religion.

In the United States, a wide range of organizations are exempt from tax. The details vary between the different states, but tax-exempt organizations generally include charitable, scientific, medical and religious organizations. On the federal level, Section 501(c) of the Internal Revenue Code gives a list of exempt organizations, which includes corporations organized and operated for religious purposes. It has been pointed out many times in legal rulings, in policy statements and in academic papers that religion is tax-exempt in the United States because it provides public benefits. Public subsidy in the form of tax-exemption is generally seen to be reasonable and even necessary to generate beneficial externalities, as it is called in economic language. In the old days, say in the eighteenth and nineteenth centuries, American religious organizations did provide many badly needed public services, like education and poor relief. Religious organizations still provide some of these services. But many do not. Government has grown enormously and filled many of the niches that religion once filled. Giving tax-exemption across the board to all religious organizations seems to rely on a somewhat old-fashioned picture of religion's role in society.

The most famous court case about tax and religion is probably *Bob Jones University versus the United States*. The case was decided in May 1983 when the Supreme Court ruled that the tax authorities (i.e. the Internal Revenue Service, IRS) had the right to revoke the tax-exempt status of Bob Jones University because of the university's racist policies. In its ruling, the Supreme Court pointed out that tax-exemption to some groups means that other taxpayers are indirect donors and that the justification for this must be "that the exempt entity confers a public benefit—a benefit which the society or the community may not itself choose or be able to provide, or which supplements and advances the work of public institutions already supported by tax revenues."[1] A racist, fundamentalist university does not strike most people as a great provider of public benefits. But the underlying assumption, seldom questioned by American courts, is the idea that religious organizations in general, despite cases like Bob Jones, actually produce public goods.

Court cases provide rich material for understanding how American society thinks about religion.[2] Let us look at the arguments about these issues in a less famous court case. In 1970, the US Supreme Court gave a ruling in a case concerning the exemption of religious organizations from property tax. The case is called *Frederick Walz versus the Tax Commission of the City of New York*. Mr Walz had gone to the Supreme Court because he believed that it went against the Constitution for the Tax Commission of the City of New York to grant churches exemption from property tax, as this indirectly forced Mr Walz, as a taxpayer, to contribute to the funding of religious bodies.

Chief Justice Burger delivered the opinion of the Supreme Court, and the text of the decision is interesting because the argument is about what kind of thing religious organizations really are. The Court started by pointing out that New York, like the other US states, had decided that certain entities that exist in a harmonious relationship to the community at large and that foster its "moral and mental improvement" shall not be inhibited by property tax. The Supreme Court decided that the state of New York was right in treating religious organizations in the same way as it treated other bodies devoted to the moral and cultural improvement of society, like libraries, charitable organizations or scientific institutes. The Supreme Court explained that the state of New York "has an affirmative policy that considers these groups as beneficial and stabilizing influences in community life ..."[3]

In order to make legal decisions concerning religion, courts are forced to say something about what they think religion is, and the general rule in US courts of law is that they see religion as something that supports the moral integrity of society and relieves government from burdensome tasks. In the decision in *Frederick Walz versus the Tax Commission of the City of New York*, the Supreme Court attempted to disentangle secular from religious reasons for exempting religious organizations from property tax. Secular purposes are welfare services, like family counseling or poor relief, and the Court argued that these kinds of services vary so much between churches that it is impossible to use "the social welfare yardstick as a significant element to qualify for tax exemption ..."[4] In the same ruling, the Supreme Court argued that subsidizing a religious organization would perhaps be a breach of the First Amendment establishment clause, but it insisted that there is a fundamental difference between the passive government support of a tax-exemption and the active support of a direct subsidy. This is a very problematic statement from an economic point of view as a tax-exemption is a type of subsidy and both types of support require government involvement.

In exchange for tax-exemption, US religious organizations must stay out of politics. The clause in the Internal Revenue Code barring all tax-exempt organizations from participating or intervening in political campaigns of any sort entered the code as part of the 1954 tax reform. The reason for this seems to have been that Lyndon B. Johnson (1908–73) wanted to bar right-wing groups from campaigning against him in Texas in his bid for re-election to the Senate.[5] Johnson would later become vice president for John F. Kennedy and then president from 1963 to 1969. In 1954, Johnson did not intend to bar churches from politics, but this was the unintended and important consequence of the tax code amendment, which prevented all tax-exempt organizations from supporting or opposing political candidates for election. This clause in the law has become important more recently as the Internal Revenue Service has tried to remove tax-exempt status from certain churches that have published views about politics in the context of presidential elections, but such clashes between government and churches have often run into the impossible issues of defining "religion" and "politics."

How much money is exempted from taxation? Americans donated roughly 115 billion US dollars to religion in 2014 and the religious sector is by far the largest recipient of charitable giving, followed by educational organizations.[6] There is little doubt that these sums are so large partly because the donors can deduct the gifts from their taxable income. But the tax forfeited on donations is only one part of the total government support to religious organizations. They receive many other public subsidies as well.

For example, in Section 107 of the Internal Revenue Code, clergy are allowed to receive either a rental home or a cash rental allowance without paying tax. It is easy to understand why lawmakers create tax-exemptions on housing for particular types of employees who are forced to live in places they do not choose themselves or have to move often as part of their job, like military personnel. But this was not the idea behind the tax-exemption for clergy-housing. If one looks at the reasoning behind Section 107, it is clear that the purpose in making this law was to advance religion, which calls into question its constitutionality.[7] There are also serious problems with how it has worked in practice. In the 1970s and early 80s an unknown number of Americans bought ordination as ministers from mail-order churches and then "donated" 50 per cent of their normal income to their own "congregation" and paid housing allowance, which can include a great variety of expenses, like furniture, gardening and local property taxes, to themselves to avoid paying tax.

This kind of shady adaption to tax regimes that grant religious organizations substantial benefits is only one element in a wider problem. The problem is that quite a few people and firms that are not actually religious label their operations as "religious" in order to receive privileges, and many religious organizations diversify into business sectors that are very far removed from the religious core of their activities. The business empires of religious leaders like the evangelical pastor Sun Myung Moon or the Hindu guru Rajneesh, which contain hotels, dairy farms, rug-cleaning ventures, pharmaceutical industries and many other lines of business that are hardly religious in any sense, are cases in point.[8] Conflicts also frequently erupt around religious movements that offer some kind of therapy without having to get the licenses and follow the strict rules of secular therapists, like medical doctors or psychologists.

Tax-exempt status would be reasonable in a religiously homogenous country in which all or most of its citizens see a national church as a public service and where they all want to use welfare services that are subsidized by government. But this type of situation has probably never existed anywhere, and it is certainly very far from the reality today as most countries become ever more diverse with more people defining themselves as belonging to minority religions or to no religion at all. Even in the United States, a country that prides itself on its separation of religion and politics, government provides substantial subsidies to religious organizations each year. The political, philosophical and legal defenses of these subsidies are all anchored in the mistaken idea that religion provides public benefits that would not have been provided without the subsidies. Religion delivers private goods, as we have seen in an earlier chapter.

The belief of many Americans that its government refrains from any involvement in the religious sector is an impressive feat of self-deception. With tens of thousands of organizations required to fill in and return the correct forms, the administration of tax-exemptions for religious bodies is a considerable job for government, but more problematic are the mounting legal cases where American courts are forced to carry out the impossible task of disentangling what is "really religious" in the activities of churches, mosques, temples and synagogues from initiatives that are essentially secular, political or pure business.

FAITHONOMICS

The idea of civil religion

Robert N. Bellah (1927–2013) was one the greatest US intellectuals of the late twentieth century. He developed the theory of civil religion in several books and articles, and although his work was mostly about the United States, his belief in the integrative powers of public religion has been picked up by thinkers on all continents and applied to societies from France to Japan. Bellah believed that all societies need a set of public and sacred beliefs and values about the social group, in modern times often a nation, expressed through shared symbols and rituals.

But the United States does not have an established church and has had a constitutional separation between religion and state for over two centuries, so how can it possibly have a public civil religion that secures national cohesion? The shared American beliefs and values that Bellah had in mind, and the rituals and symbols expressing them, do build on some very general ideas that can be traced to the Bible, like the diffuse but vaguely benign God that presidents sometimes refer to. Still, the most important symbols are not strictly religious at all, but have to do with American historical memories, like the Revolutionary War, the Constitution and the work of the Founding Fathers. Think of flag-waving children, or monuments commemorating all those who died in the great wars of the past. Exactly because they are so general these quasi-religious beliefs and values relating to history and nation can be shared by all. These sets of beliefs, values, symbols and rituals constitute civil religion. Societies that do not have this will eventually be moth-eaten by immorality and crime and disintegrate through lack of meaning and shared visions. This was Bellah's argument.

In other countries, the civil religion that is supposedly necessary for social cohesion and survival is often very closely linked to established religion. In Britain, the public role of the state church was an element in the political vision of David Cameron's government that came to power in 2010. This political vision was called the Big Society and had a focus on, among other things, creating more social cohesion and transferring power from the center to local communities. Cameron himself has repeatedly pointed out that the established church has a leading role to play in building British society. He has also said that he believes Jesus invented the Big Society and that he is simply continuing this work.[9]

A thinker who contributed to the formulation of the Big Society vision was the theologian and philosopher Phillip Blond, who wants to heal British society, which he views as having been tyrannized by Labour's big state from one side and Thatcherism's marketization from the other. The idea of a civil religion provided by the Church of England is an important part of this project because in the mind of both conservative politicians and theologians this is the only institution that has the capacity to deliver the public good they believe religion provides. This idea informs some of the publications produced by Blond's think tank ResPublica.[10]

In fact, the Big Society vision of the Tories had important religious roots in the sense that it drew some of its inspiration from association with the conservative and communitarian Christian ideas that have been developed by contemporary British theologians, like John Milbank, a professor in religion, politics and ethics at the University of Nottingham. The political ideas of conservative and communitarian theology are founded on a vision of religion as a public good. Over the past few years, secular humanists have been vocal in their criticism of Prime Minister David Cameron's references to Christianity and to the Church of England and other faith organizations as partners in tackling social problems in Great Britain. Elizabeth O'Casey, who is a key person in the National Secular Society, wrote that Cameron's "courting of Christianity" was divisive, cynical and shallow, and other secular humanists have criticized the British prime minister in similar terms.[11]

Be sociable, or get out

How could public intellectuals with serious political influence like Robert N. Bellah in the United States and Phillip Blond in the UK get it so wrong? The misunderstanding started with a Frenchman. In 1762, the philosopher Jean-Jacques Rousseau published a book—*The Social Contract*—that would become extremely important for how later generations would think about society and the place of individuals in it.

"Man is born free, and everywhere he is in chains." This is the powerful first sentence of Rousseau's book, a major work in European political philosophy. The author is concerned with human freedom and believes that an ideal society will in fact preserve and promote such freedom. Rousseau was fundamentally opposed to the Hobbesian vision of human nature. Hobbes thought that the state of nature was all against all in a state of war. Rousseau was a romantic who believed that man before society would have roamed around in a relatively carefree state—eating berries and honey, perhaps, and greeting passersby with a smile—without any inclination to violence. Human beings come together and make a social contract in order to achieve a kind of freedom that is higher and better than that achieved on their own.

The basis for society for Rousseau is something called the general will. The general will is not the sum total of the will of all individuals. It is rather a new and higher order of will that comes into existence when people come together and establish society. Those forming society do not cease to be individual persons, of course, but in society a new kind of person is born, the collective person. This collective person, called the body politic, is a real, moral being possessed of a will of its own and it always wants to act in the best interest of the whole. Most of the time, the welfare of the whole will be consistent with the welfare and needs of individual members, but certainly not always. Sometimes, individual members of society, or groups of individuals, will have selfish interests that are inconsistent with the general will. Part of the trick of politics is to find ways to solve such conflicts. Rousseau finds the answer in civil religion.

In the last chapter of *The Social Contract*, he writes that there is a purely civil profession of faith of which the sovereign—the king or the government—should fix the articles. These articles are not exactly religious dogmas, he says, but rather social sentiments without which a man cannot be a good citizen or faithful subject. While government can compel no one to believe in these dogmas, it can banish from the state anyone who does not believe in them because he is an anti-social being, incapable of truly loving the laws and unwilling to sacrifice his life for his duty to the collective. Rousseau lists the basic elements:

> The dogmas of the civil religion must be simple and few, precisely expressed, without explanations or commentary. The existence of the Divinity, powerful, intelligent, beneficent,

prescient, and provident, the life to come, the reward of the just and the punishment of the wicked, the holiness of the laws and the social contract; such are the positive dogmas.[12]

So Rousseau insisted that a diffuse monotheism infused with a huge dose of sanctified social identification and commitment is the true religion of the good society. He is very clear on this point. Either you submit to this civil religion, or you leave. If you first accept these general dogmas and then break them, the state should kill you on behalf of the general will.

Rousseau's idea about society being a collective person with a will of its own opens the door to totalitarianism. Although it is different from the tyranny arising from Hobbes's vision, it is still worrying from the point of view of political liberalism. There is also a paradox here because Rousseau contributed to the romantic movement, which criticized civilization and idealized nature and the individual. Rousseau was a difficult man. He was suspicious and quarreled even with people who believed in his ideas and supported him. Because of all the trouble he caused in the salons of Paris in the 1750s and 60s, and because his work was officially banned, he escaped to England in 1766 where he received generous help from the great Scottish philosopher David Hume, whom we met in an earlier chapter. But let us move on and look at the ideas of a much later Frenchman.

It's the anthropologists' fault

The idea of religion as a public good received an important modern philosophical expression in the work of Rousseau, but its firm support in mainstream social science was established much later. The founder of modern social science, Émile

Durkheim (1858–1917), believed he had made a great discovery when, in a classic book called *The Elementary Forms of Religious Life* (1912), he launched the idea that societies actually worship themselves when they pray, dance and sacrifice to the gods. The idea had matured over some time. In 1895, Durkheim read the work of the Scottish professor, William Robertson Smith, who was an expert on the ancient religion of the peoples who spoke Semitic languages, like Arabic and Hebrew.[13] Durkheim himself describes this as a revelation. The historical study of religion that Durkheim discovered in the books of Smith revealed to him that religion was about sacred things and that it was about the social group and not about the beliefs and ideas of the individual.

This does not sound too original, perhaps, but don't forget that Durkheim lived in a time when religion had mostly been talked about and studied as individual beliefs or emotions. Since the Reformation, Europeans had tended to think of Christianity as the face-to-face encounter with God and the lonely responsibility for right belief. Bringing the social nature of religion into focus the way Durkheim did was an innovation in the late nineteenth and early twentieth century.

Already at the very beginning of his career as a scholar—his first article appeared in 1885—Durkheim was convinced that social facts had an existence that was fundamentally different from the sum of the thoughts and actions of the individuals that made up a group of people. He believed that societies had something he called social conscience or collective spirit, which was supposed to be a compound of all individual consciences or spirits. In Durkheim's mind, such a collective spirit was necessary for people to feel any kind of moral obligation to each other and it was therefore the foundation of society. All moral codes and laws were strictly social. The very glue of society was the almost mystical higher collective spirit that was produced when people live together in groups.

Since these kinds of social facts have a very real existence, it is absolutely necessary, Durkheim argued, to study them in a different way than we study individual facts. If you believe you can grasp the collective consciousness of groups by studying the psychological processes of individuals, you are badly mistaken. Such statements about method and perspective would be the foundation on which to build the new science of society: sociology. The individuals making up society contribute to creating the collective spirit, but they are not aware of this themselves. So ignorance was part of the equation. This was another foundational myth of Durkheim's branch of sociology. All the social stuff, like morality and religion, seems to hover around in the air above the heads of real people, but they are not able to see through the social processes that produce it. According to Durkheimian thinking, this stuff has functions that are necessary for social cohesion and survival, but these functions remain hidden to members of society.

Hovering above most human societies is one or several gods, which, according to Durkheim, is just a symbol of society itself. When people worship gods, they worship their own society without knowing it. Durkheim was interested in religion because he believed it was at the heart of social life. To make the final statement about his ideas he rounded off his career with a book called *The Elementary Forms of Religious Life*, a classic in the academic study of religion mostly built on examples from Australian aboriginal religion. Durkheim never went to Australia, but for unclear reasons most people at that time assumed that Australian totemism was religion in its most primitive form.

The idea that Durkheim planted securely at the heart of academic, social and political debate in Europe was that all societies must have religion in some form, or they will fall apart. These ideas were developed further by other sociologists and anthropologists who were thinking in the same terms. The great British anthropologist A. R. Radcliffe-Brown (1881–1945) was probably the most important in the generation after Durkheim. Radcliffe-Brown did extensive fieldwork in several parts of the world, something Durkheim never did, and he taught anthropology for a long time both at the University of Chicago and later at the University of Oxford, exerting enormous influence on the development of anthropology in both America and Britain.

Is society a body?

Radcliffe-Brown compared society to a body. He looked at social institutions and tried to determine their function for society as a whole. Religion was one of the institutions that interested him: religious practice has a function in society, he insisted. In an important essay called "Religion and Society," presented in 1945 as the prestigious Henry Myers Lecture, Radcliffe-Brown explained that anthropologists have to look beyond the contents and beyond superficial questions about the truth or falsehood of religious beliefs.[14] The student of religion should focus on the rituals and their functions in society. This approach was in itself important at the time because much of the writing about religion in the Western world was nothing more than polemical defenses of "true religion"—Christianity—and attacks on the primitive ideas of "savages." In Radcliffe-Brown's thinking, religion performs functions that are necessary to preserve the social organism, and as societies are built differently, so religious systems will vary according to how they perform the role of expressing and keeping alive certain human feelings that are necessary for social integration. In war, for instance, religious rites will bolster feelings of patriotism, as they had in Germany in the horrible conflict that had just ended when he was giving his talk about religion and society.

Radcliffe-Brown was deeply influenced by Durkheim and he supported Durkheim's idea about the social functions of religious rites among Australian aborigines.[15] The direction of social scientific thought represented by Radcliffe-Brown is known as structural-functionalism, and although later social scientists have criticized the approach, the appealing but mistaken idea that society is an organism with institutions that are necessary for continued existence, like the organs or limbs of a body, continues to exert influence on both scholars and the public.

Here we have the basic thought behind the belief that religion is a public good. I have traced the belief back to the philosopher Rousseau and to Durkheim, the founding father of sociology, and to A.R. Radcliffe-Brown, a key thinker in modern anthropology. Rousseau, Durkheim and Radcliffe-Brown argued that society is a body, they believed that all its members are parts of this living whole and that participating in common religious rites or ceremonies is necessary to produce something they would describe as a collective spirit or social sentiments. We should not lose sight of the fact that the academic writings of both Rousseau and Durkheim were highly value-laden and normative—Radcliffe-Brown's less so. The two Frenchmen were incredibly intelligent observers of the world, but they also had very strong ideas about how we should organize society. There was nothing neutral about their research. The problem is that their often quite vague ideas about things like social sentiments and social cohesion are still very much alive today. Many people now accept Durkheim's idea that religions are important contributors to a public good that is often talked of as "social cohesion" or "social integration" or "moral order." Quite a few scholars also believe that religion provides some sort of public good in the sense that it creates order through the fear of punishment in the afterlife.[16] To see how these thoughts are translated into actual policy, we can take a look at the emergence of a European debate about religious education in public schools.

A soul for Europe

Modern education serves several purposes, one of which is to create some common understanding of society and its norms and expectations. In Europe, there have been growing concerns about how children and adolescents should learn about religion over the past decade or so. Jacques Delors, the highly influential president of the European Commission from 1985 to 1995, talked about the urgency of creating a soul for Europe through religious education.

These concerns are partly the result of the project of European integration, which is challenged by several things, among them religious pluralization. But these concerns are perhaps even more a result of the increasing global awareness of religion as a political force, especially after 9/11 and other terrorist attacks in the Western world. In the EU, there has been a major policy shift in the sense that European intergovernmental institutions started advocating the study of religion in public schools as a way to avoid violent conflict and create the conditions for social cohesion.[17]

One indication that religious education is increasingly seen as a sensitive issue closely connected with matters of national security was the recommendations made in the "Toledo Guiding Principles on Teaching about Religions and Beliefs in Public Schools," which was published by the Organization for Security and Co-operation in Europe (OSCE). The OSCE originated as a forum facilitating security dialogue between the Western world and the Communist bloc in the 1970s. It now comprises fifty-seven states throughout Europe and Central Asia as well as the United States. The Toledo Guiding Principles recommend that public schools in the organization's area should teach religion with an eye to enhancing social cohesion and reducing conflicts.[18]

The EU has also taken initiatives addressing the topic of religious education in public schools in Europe and they have all rested on explicit ideas about the need for some kind of common European understanding of and approach to questions of faith that can create a common civil religion. Speeches and documents outlining these initiatives often assume that if Europe is able to inculcate the right ideas and values on religious matters in new generations of kids, the continent will have a better chance of avoiding conflicts and be successful in its project of political and economic integration.

In 2008, for example, the Council of Europe completed a project on the teaching of religion in Europe and issued a recommendation by the Committee of Ministers, the foreign ministers of the forty-seven member states, giving a number of principles that members should bear in mind when designing future education policies.[19] The recommendation saw religious education in the larger framework of an inter-cultural approach to education that should promote respect for religious diversity, would help children overcome prejudices and would contribute to the development of societies based on solidarity. The recommendation was fairly detailed on some points, for instance when calling for a phenomenological and interpretative approach to the teaching of religion.

Policy initiatives in the EU were followed up by research. The largest research project designed to come up with data to support such initiatives was carried out between 2006 and 2009, and is known by its acronym REDCo (short for "Religion in Education: A Contribution to Dialogue or a Factor of Conflict in Transforming Societies of European Countries?"). REDCo was coordinated by Professor Wolfram Weisse at the University of Hamburg and involved scholars from a wide range of European countries. They worked to map and compare the potentials and limitations of religious education in the school systems of the different states in Europe and gain a better understanding of how religious education might contribute to fostering mutual respect and creating a collective European identity.

Some of the scholars involved in the REDCo research project wrote about a European civil religion as a goal of religious education in public schools. Although often formulated only in vague terms, they tended to see European states moving into a phase of religious education where the hegemony of Christianity was broken and where a new collective identity could be built by teachers if they conveyed knowledge and values about religion in the right way.[20]

The goals of mutual respect and understanding expressed both in European policy initiatives and in research are clearly something to which we should aspire. The problem is that in the talking and writing about the teaching of religion in public schools we find the lingering presence of the ideas about civil religion that I have criticized in this chapter. Many of the leading politicians driving these initiatives talk about religious education as a tool for creating a collective European identity and social cohesion. This necessarily entails politicizing religion and religious education in Europe. Many are concerned about the fact that religion is increasingly securitized after 9/11, which means that religion is talked about more and more in terms of security. It is an aspect of the deepening securitization of religion that European politicians and scholars have started to see the public teaching of religion in member states primarily as a tool to avoid violent conflict and create social cohesion. They are committing the same errors as earlier scholars I have mentioned, like the great sociologist Durkheim, who was deeply worried that modern society had become so complex and fragmented that it needed unifying ideas, values and symbols—a civil religion—if the social organism was going to survive. The trouble with this approach is that it legitimizes government interference in what schools should tell children about religion and it is quite likely that this leads to bias or even misrepresentation of religion in schools, which may again be perceived as unwarranted state interference by religious groups.[21]

PART 2

HISTORY—RELIGIOUS MARKETS IN OTHER TIMES AND PLACES

5

RELIGIOUS MARKETS IN ISLAM

The main objection against the application of the economic perspective to religion is to say that it presupposes a modern and specifically Protestant idea of religion, which is foreign to other religions and to other periods of history. Steve Bruce, a sociologist and one of the staunchest critics of the economic perspective on religion, has argued that people generally do not see religions as interchangeable like cars or other commodities. Religions demand and get the complete faith of their adherents, Bruce claims.[1] The idea that modern Protestantism is the only religion in which adherents are able to see religious affiliation as a personal choice has come to dominate the work of both the critics and the defenders of the approach.

If this criticism is correct, it should be easy to observe the religious life of other civilizations and find out that religion there has been constituted in radically different ways from modern Protestantism. We would find that in all pre-modern societies religion is so intertwined with culture and tradition that it would be meaningless to talk about religious goods as substitutes and about individual believers as consumers who have a choice in where they want to turn for their religious goods. In particular, for religions to be substitutes for each other in a market, religion must be separated from culture, critics claim, and this separation is something uniquely modern and something specifically American. Steve Bruce insists that the only kind of society in which the economic perspective on religion might work would be a society where religion was detached from tradition and culture (i.e. a society in which religion no longer matters).[2]

Olivier Roy, an expert on Islam and a well-known commentator on modern religion, claims that what is special about religion in a modern and globalized world is that it has been separated from culture. This separation makes it possible for modern people to experiment and choose religious identities in completely new ways and independently of cultural codes and constraints, he says. Roy argues that the emergence of a market approach to religion among modern believers goes hand in hand with a process he calls deculturation: religion becomes detached from culture in order to be marketable.[3]

In the introduction, I explained that I have a political motivation for writing this book alongside purely intellectual curiosity. I described a network of scholars who attack Western initiatives for international religious freedom. These scholars believe there is a conspiracy behind religious freedom work. They claim that Western governments and diplomats, aided by scholarship in economics and other disciplines, are seeking to impose an understanding of religion as a marketplace throughout the world. This is a way to prepare the ground for the Christian mission, they believe. After Muslims, Buddhists, Hindus and the rest of the "non-West" have been forced to believe in the idea that religion is something that should be chosen freely according to individual conscience, a range of evangelical and fundamentalist Christian missionary organizations will be free to capture this new market with their superior resources. I do not need to point out that I strongly disagree with this perspective. We should talk about and criticize cases where Western governments are implicated in aggressive campaigns of proselytization in vulnerable societies. But let us not forget that religious freedom is a human right that most states agree on and this includes the right to proselytize.

The four chapters in this part of the book are written to show that those who insist that economic perspectives on religion are relevant only in the modern West are wrong. By looking at some examples from four very different historical contexts, I will show that it is possible—and indeed reasonable—to identify markets for religion far outside the Christian context and long before modern times. If you already agree that the economic approach to religion is more or less universally applicable, and if you are easily bored by the history of religions, you may want to skip this part and go directly to Part 3, where the ideas are applied to today's political realities. But if you still need some convincing that the market perspective has universal relevance, please take time to read what follows below.

The classic religious oligopoly

The world of Islam stretches from Morocco in the west to Indonesia in the east and contains incredibly diverse societies and cultures. In modern thinking about religion, the Islamic world is never understood from the perspective of the economics of religion. The fact is, however, that most Islamic societies in history have harbored markets for religion.

Islamic societies have varied considerably in their political organization and administration. Most journalists, and quite a few scholars, have come to hold the idea that Islamic societies never differentiated between state and religion. Already from the ninth century there emerged a deep institutional split between political and religious structures, and between the professionals who defined these fields. The struggle for authority in the field of religion was settled once and for all when the Abbasid *caliphs* of the mid-ninth century gave up their campaign to define the nature of the Quran and accepted that the religious scholars (*ulama*), and not the *caliph*, were the legitimate interpreters of holy scripture. Many Islamic societies after this formative period would build the division of religion and politics into their institutions of government.[4]

If we insist on talking about religious life with the simplistic label "world religions," we might look for religious markets comprising, say, Islam, Judaism and different branches of Christianity. But we would search in vain for evidence of real competition between these traditions. A typical Islamic state worked as a religious oligopoly because the state recognized a certain number of religious societies with their own religious organizations and leaderships. The state regulated the religious market and there was little or no real competition between the officially recognized religious groups and their religious organizations.

One brief example: the center of learning in the Sunni Islamic world is the great university called al-Azhar in Cairo with its adjoining mosque. Al-Azhar was founded by the Caliph al-Muizz, who ruled the Fatimid Empire of North Africa from 953 to 975. The Fatimid Empire was founded in AD 909 in the area that is now Tunisia and parts of Algeria, and over the next two centuries it expanded and developed into an Islamic state that exerted great influence in the

Mediterranean region and in the Hijaz, the western parts of the Arabian peninsula. When the Fatimids expanded eastward and invaded Egypt, the first thing they did was to found the city of Cairo and establish a great mosque and a university. The name al-Azhar refers to Fatima, the daughter of Muhammad and the wife of Ali, Muhammad's cousin and son-in-law. The Fatimids were Shia Muslims who believed that the rightful leaders of the Muslim community must belong to the descendants of Fatima and Ali. They belonged to the branch of Shia Islam called Ismaili or Seveners, as opposed to the Twelvers, the main branch in Iran. This meant that the Fatimid ruling class were a religious minority governing a highly diverse population of Sunni Muslims, Khariji Muslims, Coptic Christians, Jews and other people.

The Fatimid rulers created a system of governance of religious diversity where some degree of competition between religious groups was tolerated by the government. This pragmatic governance of religious diversity seems to have been part of a larger trend in this period. During the tenth century, there developed a great degree of religious plurality in the Middle East and the main reason for this was the splintering of Shia groups and the creation of Shia states. There was a political and cultural renaissance where a wide range of Islamic religiosities flourished, as well as Hellenistic philosophies and even secularist ideas. The Fatimid Empire illustrates the religious diversity that many Islamic empires have harbored. In typical Islamic societies, the state supported Islamic institutions and kept some control over religious elites, while other religious communities, like Jews or Christians of different dominations, kept their own religious cultures, norms and rituals.

The people of an Islamic state would have a religious identity ascribed to them by family and community, and sometimes by government, and there would be little scope and few incentives for changing these identities. Ascribed identities are those that are given to somebody at birth or at some stage in early life. They are inherited and more or less immutable. Some degree of conversion to Islam might happen, but this is not the level of analysis that is relevant if we want to understand Islamic societies as religious markets. But ascribed identities (i.e. identities as Muslim or Jew or Christian) were not the only kind of religious identity that people had. Many would also have a range of possible achieved religious identities, and the most important area by far to look for an understanding of such identities in Islam is the world of Sufism.

Sufism and religious markets in Islam

Official religion is expressed in the Sharia as the legal framework for maintaining social harmony and individual morality. The scholars educated in legal science (*fiqh*), and trusted with keeping up the intergenerational legal discussion of law, morality and right conduct that is Sharia were embodiments of official religion. But all societies where Islam became state religion would also harbor a great number of different practices, rituals and beliefs that we can call popular or non-official religion and these would exist alongside official religion. For instance, many people would believe in ghosts and spirits and would perform rituals to appease such powers. After the pioneering work of the historian and classicist James G. Frazer (1854–1941), scholars of religion tend to keep the concepts of magic and religion very much apart, but in reality the boundaries between religion and magic were not always so clear.

Sufism is the most important aspect of religion to look at for an understanding of Islamic religious markets. Sufism is met with in the Western world today through the famous *qawwali* songs of Nusrat Fateh Ali Khan, easily enjoyed from any streaming service, or the best-selling English translations of the poetry of the thirteenth-century Persian poet Rumi. But Sufism is a wide variety of religious ideas, practices and styles that have in various ways dominated Islamic societies.

The word "Sufism" is often translated as "Islamic mysticism," which is only partly right because Sufi practice and ritual have often been more communal affairs than the individual meditation on God that we associate with mysticism. Sufism as a path towards experiencing God was present in Islam from the very earliest times. The key ingredient was the bond between a teacher and a pupil. Students received training in loosely organized residential centers that developed around charismatic teachers. Training focused more on experience than on knowledge. From the twelfth century AD, the paths or brotherhoods (*tariqas*) developed into institutions with their own initiatory traditions and distinctive styles of religiosity. Some of the most important are the Qadiri, the Chishti, the Mevlevi and the Naqshbandi, which were founded or inspired by Sufi masters of the twelfth to fourteenth centuries.[5] I will return to the Naqshbandi brotherhood in a discussion of modern Turkey.

The importance of Sufi Brotherhoods to Islamic societies went far beyond the purely religious. Often, the shaykhs and their brotherhoods would play important political roles, as when the Sufi scholar, warrior and religious revivalist Muhammad b. Ali al-Sanusi (1787–1859) established a new and important brotherhood—the Sanusi or Senussi order—and at the same time fought French and Italian colonial forces in North Africa and laid the foundations for the Kingdom of Libya, which lasted until Gaddafi's coup in 1969.[6] We could have listed other historical cases where Sufi orders played significant political or social roles, but let us get back to our main focus: the religious markets of Islam.

Religious markets in Islamic societies consisted of the supply of religious goods offered by the Sufi shaykhs and their networks of followers. For the argument in this book, the importance of Sufi brotherhoods and the networks they have created in Islamic societies lies in the fact that they offered a type of religious identity that was achieved rather than ascribed by birth. True, a family or a clan would often associate itself with a local Sufi tradition and a child would be socialized into the world of the local Sufi shaykh through, for instance, Quran-readings at the local Sufi house and at rituals such as name-giving and circumcision. However, the attachment to a brotherhood was something that could be chosen by the adult individual. He or she could seek out a new shaykh or leave an old one for a number of different reasons, and the popularity of a Sufi teacher could go up or down, his following could grow or shrink or simply dry out.[7] For the affiliate or full member of a brotherhood, religious identity was achieved in the sense that it required initiation and long periods of training through many stages. The seriously interested seeker of religious insight would be free to receive initiation and training in different brotherhoods in his search for the right teacher and the best training. People who were religiously inclined could shop around.

For common people, the religious goods offered by Sufi brotherhoods, such as rituals, healing and welfare services, were often very important. The Sufi shaykh would cater to the religious needs of common people, something the legalistic Islam of the scholars (*ulama*) could not always do. For many people, and especially for women, regular visits to the tombs of the saints were more important than official prayer in mosques. Very often the elites of official religion would also take part in the non-official religion supplied by the Sufi brotherhoods and most of the time people did not see any contradiction in the fact that a highly educated legal scholar would also be an initiate in a Sufi brotherhood. Sufi shaykhs could have very different styles. Some were sober and intellectual and offered philosophical explanations of passages of scripture, while others lived in states of ecstatic intoxication. The shaykhs and the Sufi brotherhoods forming around them catered to a wide range of different religious demands in a population and they were often quite accessible to common people.

Sufism has had a rough ride in modern times, especially from the end of the nineteenth century. It is a common assumption in research on Islam that the modern Muslim mindset is characterized by a tendency to search for an Islam that is purified from its entanglements with popular religious expressions like Sufism. Many of the Islamic reform movements that started in the nineteenth century, and which sought to make Islam more comfortable with modern worldviews like science and secular education, perceived Sufism as an obstacle to progress. The relationship between Sufism and the modern movements that we call fundamentalist is also ambivalent and often hostile. Perhaps the most important Muslim fundamentalist intellectual of all, Maulana Maududi (1903–79), strongly denounced Sufism. The prominent Egyptian radical Sayyid Qutb was of the same opinion. In fact, in most Islamic societies one can find disparaging attitudes towards Sufism among some people.

These conflicts are evident in Indonesia, for example, the largest Muslim nation in the world. In the densely populated island of Java, where the Indonesian capital Jakarta is located, several different styles of religion are common. In particular, there is a clear distinction, and sometimes tension, between what is known as Agami Jawi and Santri. Agami Jawi is very common in the countryside and is a mix of Islamic, Hindu and animistic elements. A few decades ago, social scientists would have called Agami Jawi a "syncretic" system because it mixes different traditions. Today, nobody uses the term "syncretism" because we are no longer comfortable with the idea that we can identify pure religions that are mixed with other pure religions, like ingredients in a cake.

Santri, however, is a more self-consciously pure Islam, and those who identify with this religious style reject Hinduism and animism. Santri is associated with strict performance of Islamic rituals and an emphasis on doctrinal understanding. As Java and Indonesia modernize, it seems that the balance between the mixed folk religion and the self-consciously pure and strict Islam is changing. The tendency has been for people with higher education and urban lifestyles in Java to reject the folk religion expressed in Agami Jawi and embrace what they see as the "purer" religion of Santri. This desire to purify Islam seems to be a consequence of modern, secular education and urbanization.[8]

Religious identity

My argument is that Islamic societies everywhere have always had at least two systems of religion that have overlapped and interacted in complex ways. Muslims throughout history have lived lives where some elements of their religious identities have been achieved rather than ascribed and innate. In the social sciences, it is a standard assumption that pre-modern and modern societies differ fundamentally in the way they shape people's identities. The classic thinkers in social science, like Émile Durkheim, whom we met in an earlier chapter, were certain that the roles and identities that people have in pre-modern societies—or primitive or traditional societies, as they often called them—were a matter of ascription, which means they are given to you by family, clan, tribe or society. In modern societies, on the other hand, the roles and identities people have are not ascribed, but rather achieved by their own actions and aspirations. Ascribed identities are inherited and they are fixed and stable, while achieved identities are fluid and open. Achieved identities and roles make modern societies open and free.

In the sphere of religion, this means that modern societies open up for religious choice. People can shop around for the religious supplier they like and they are far less constrained by the religious identities with which they are born. This does not mean that people constantly switch between Christianity, Judaism, Islam and Buddhism. Far more relevant are the types of affiliations and identities people choose for themselves within these large, overarching religious traditions. Protestants in the United States can change membership of churches and denominations more easily than their grandparents could. Jews are still born with a Jewish identity that most people see as ascribed, but the types of Jewish beliefs and practices (or non-beliefs or non-practices) they choose for themselves are probably more a matter of choice now than was the case some generations ago.

Some lament the individualism that goes hand in hand with achieved identities because they see it as a threat to social cohesion and stability. Others rejoice in the modern condition of individualism and freedom. But there are serious problems with the way the concepts of achieved and ascribed roles and identities are used to grasp the differences between modern and pre-modern, new and old. For a start, nobody really knows when the thing they call "modernity" actually started. The word was used in the Middle Ages to talk about old-fashioned people that lived before; for some reason everybody seems to think that they are the moderns. Ask a hundred historians, and you may not get a hundred completely different answers, but I bet you get at least ten. Yet a criticism that is more to the point is that societies in "the old days," in pre-modern times as it were, had systems of religion where people achieved their roles and identities by their own individual efforts, like Sufism.

I think we should see ascription and achievement as endpoints on a scale rather than two mutually exclusive categories. A religious identity can be inherited without being utterly immutable and it may be up to an individual whether and to what extent he or she is interested in achieving new roles by, for instance, taking a more active role in a congregation or by taking initiation with, for example, a Sufi shaykh in Islam or a guru in India. Let me be clear. I think it is a fundamental failure of the social scientific study of religion that it has failed to see that quite a few religious roles and identities found in so-called pre-modern societies have been achieved, and not ascribed. The religious systems that are open to individual choices—where men (and sometimes women) can achieve different statuses and acquire identities that they were not born into—have in fact constituted religious markets in the Islamic world throughout history. Sufism is the best example of such a system.

Ottoman oligopoly

The Ottoman Empire lasted from 1299 to 1923 and is the longest-surviving empire in history. It offers a classic case of how a pre-modern Islamic state governed a bewildering ethnic and religious diversity, which included Orthodox Greek, Romanian and Bulgarian Christians, as well as Catholics in Hungary and Croatia, and Sephardi and Ashkenazi Jews, and many other communities who were in charge of their own educational, cultural and legal affairs. Even more importantly, it offers a classic case of what happens when an old imperial model breaks down and is replaced by nationalist and republican values and modern institutions of government.

Unfortunately, the history of Islamic societies has been wildly politicized in recent decades. Historical writing about the Ottoman Empire has become a battleground in this war of words, which means that everything one says or writes about it may be read as a political statement. Many historians see the Ottoman period as a great example of harmony between social groups and between state and society, a model to be followed, while other observers focus on what they see as oppression of minorities and arbitrary rule. In the most rabid exchanges, historical examples are marshaled to argue for or against the inherent evil of Islam. I do not want to engage in this kind of meaningless debate. The Ottoman order was a system that provided relatively strong protections for the rights of groups and individuals, but there were also episodes of forced conversions or large-scale movements of communities against their will. Non-Muslims paid a special tax and could not testify against Muslims in a Muslim court, and they did not have access to the very highest offices of the state throughout much of Ottoman history.

In many of the popular histories about the Ottomans one can read about the *millet* system. The *millet* system was a socio-political order according to which each of the major non-Muslim religious communities of the Ottoman Empire was allowed to rule its own legal and cultural affairs. However, historians now doubt that the *millet* system was the result of a grand plan in the management of religious and ethnic diversity and one could question the very idea that it was a consistent system at all. It seems more reasonable to understand the *millet* system rather as an order that came into being in a piecemeal fashion as each community was granted its rights and its freedoms in an ad hoc manner.

The technical term for non-Muslims living inside the Islamic state, *dhimmi* and *dhimmihood*, has been a political and legal subject for Islamic political leaders and for Islamic scholars through the history of Islam. The early jurists argued about exactly who was to be counted as *dhimmi* and receive the special protection and duties extended to religious minorities within the Islamic community. Jews and Christians were always regarded as *dhimmis*, but there was more uncertainty regarding Zoroastrians and non-Muslim Arab minorities. *Dhimmis* were protected, but they also had to pay a special tax, the *jizya*, and most jurists were of the opinion that they should abide by Islamic law in some areas of life. The reality was often far more complex and policies often more pragmatic in the different regions where Muslim rulers governed non-Muslims.

The Ottomans inherited the thinking about *dhimmis* from earlier Islamic political ideology. Both Muslims and non-Muslims were organized in groups or communities that were in the last instance answerable to the caliph. The Muslim masses were subdivided according to schools of law or affiliation with different Sufi brotherhoods and the leaders of these were responsible to the state as representatives of their groups. The Ottomans brought the religious institutions and the religious elites under bureaucratic control and much of the economic life of the Ottoman era was organized along ethnic or religious lines. (Ethnic and religious identities were often the same, or overlapping, and these modern terms do not help us very much in describing the pre-modern situation.) Sometimes, the control of trade was divided according to religious groups by commodity. For example, in the Ottoman Balkan heartlands of the late sixteenth century, Muslims controlled a share of the trade in foodstuff that was out of proportion to their numerical strength, while Christians controlled almost all of the trade in wine. Christians controlled the trade in imported woolen cloth, while Muslims controlled the trade in home-made woolen cloth. The different communities—Muslims, Christians and Jews—specialized in trade in different types of leather products. These ethno-religious groups formed cartels that worked to keep the price of their products artificially high.[9]

Just as the religious groups were granted certain rights in trade and built networks and cartels within the legal frameworks of the empire, so they worked in practice as organizations with a near monopoly within their own niche of the religious market. This means that from the point of view of the economics of religion, the Ottoman system seems to be the perfect case of an oligopolistic model, where a strong state decides on a certain number of organizations that can supply goods and services.

Neo-Ottoman free market?

In Turkey, the start of the twentieth century was marked by violent political upheaval and wide-ranging transformations in the relationship between Islam and the state. The Ottoman Empire weakened dramatically throughout the nineteenth century, and the twentieth century started out with a series of political and military disasters for the Turks. In 1911 and 1912, the Ottomans fought Italy and lost its territories along the Libyan coast as well as the Dodecanese, the strategically important group of islands just outside the Turkish coast in the South Aegean Sea.

The Balkan Wars in 1912 and 1913 resulted in the loss of Ottoman lands in southeastern Europe and an enormous influx of Muslim refugees into the heartland of the empire in Asia escaping persecution by the new Orthodox Christian rulers of the Balkans. The First World War saw the Ottoman sultan ally himself with Germany in 1914 in the hope of recapturing former Ottoman territory and halting Russia's expansion in the Caucasus. The Ottomans ended up on the losing side of the Great War. Formerly Ottoman lands in the Middle East were carved up by the Allies and were taken as protectorates by British and French forces. The Turkish National Movement emerged as a response to the humbling defeat and the Turkish War of Independence from 1919 to 1922 ended with the recognition of the Turkish Republic in the Treaty of Lausanne in July 1923. The nationalist leader Mustafa Kemal Atatürk (1881–1938) was the first president of the Turkish Republic.

Atatürk was inspired by European, particularly French, secularist ideology and saw traditional Turkish Islam, and traditional forms of religion in general, as an obstacle to progress and modernization. The Kemalists embarked on a massive program of de-Islamization. Sufism was banned in 1925. The officially accepted form of Islam was brought under strict government control through the establishment of the

Directorate of Religious Affairs, which soon changed its name to the Presidency of Religious Affairs (often referred to by its shortened Turkish name: the Diyanet).

The Diyanet is the branch of government in Turkey responsible for the organization and maintenance of mosques, the employment of religious personnel throughout the country and a number of other activities. During the first decades of the Turkish Republic, the strict secularist regime meant that non-official versions and expressions of Islam were banned. The Sufi brotherhoods were dismantled and their networks, which had been such an essential element in Turkish social life throughout the Ottoman period, were driven underground. The Kemalist authorities justified these anti-Sufi campaigns by referring to their subversive political role in Turkish politics, and arrested, and even killed, some prominent Sufi shaykhs. Although the Turkish authorities certainly exaggerated the dangers posed by supposedly seditious Sufi brotherhoods, these were not always completely groundless accusations as the Sufi orders, especially the Naqshbandis, did in fact organize political disturbances to protest against the repression of Islam in secular Turkey. The Turkish government sought to replace mosques and Sufi communal houses (*tekke*) with People's Houses in cities and towns where people were encouraged to take part in secular activities. In other words, the state sought to crowd out traditional religion by supplying secular substitutes in the form of new places of social and communal life, new rituals and the secular worship of the Turkish nation and its great father, Atatürk.

From the establishment of the Turkish Republic in 1923 to the Second World War, Turkish secularism was oppressive—this period was characterized by the Kemalists' insistence on national homogeneity and the efforts of the

Directorate of Religious Affairs to enforce a religious monopoly that was bent on creating a hegemonic conception of Islam and enacting a strict privatization of religious life. Such grand state projects are seldom successful in the long run. Like other monopolies, it probably led to reduced consumption of religion among many Turks and it certainly caused resentment, although certain minorities, like the Alevis, sought to ally themselves with the secularist state.

Deep transformations have taken place in Turkey's policies regarding religion since the death of Atatürk and especially after the Second World War. From the 1950s, the persecution and repression of religion by the Kemalists started to lessen and, gradually, room for diverse religious expression started to expand. A period of rapid change set in with the political leadership of Turgut Özal, a popular and liberal-minded politician who was prime minister from 1983 to 1989 and then president from 1989 to his death in 1993. Özal was a successful businessman and a practicing Muslim with ties to the Naqshbandi Sufi order.

The Naqshbandi order has played a fascinating role in Turkish political life over the last three or four decades. The rise of Islamist political parties in Turkey is closely associated with the prominent Sufi Shaykh Mehmed Zahid Kotku (1897–1980) who was the spiritual teacher to several of the most important Turkish politicians of the past forty years. The National Order Party and the National Salvation Party of Necmettin Erbakan (1926–2011) grew out of the Naqshbandi milieu around Kotku. Erbakan was a major force in Turkish politics who would go on to form the Welfare Party and serve as prime minister from 1996 to 1997. Recep Tayyip Erdogan, Turkish prime minister between 2003 and 2014 and currently the country's president, was also a pupil of Kotku. Both Turgut Özal and his younger brother Korkut Özal were pupils of the legendary Sufi shaykh, and in a very personal essay published in 1999, Korkut Özal, a professor and former minister of agriculture, related his experience as a Sufi initiate in Kotku's order.[10] Kotku was a religious leader, but he was also a modern thinker and activist who wanted his disciples to get engaged in politics, business and industry.

The religious networks among top business leaders and academics that formed around Kotku provided Turgut Özal with the perfect base for politics and helped his Motherland Party win a landslide victory in the 1983 elections. Özal was the architect of the liberalization of Turkey's economy, which helped the country out of its deep economic crisis of the 1970s. He and his government have been criticized for overlooking the fact that a well-functioning market-economy needs to be governed by robust institutional structures and transparent and predictable rules, but there is little doubt that the reforms they started were largely welcome and led to rapid economic growth.[11]

On matters of culture and religion, the reforms that were carried out under Özal from the mid-1980s had important consequences for Turkey's religious and cultural development. Özal had lived in the United States and was convinced that America's success owed a great deal to its liberal policies. He wanted to reshape the Turkish state to allow for public expressions of different forms of religion and culture, including Kurdish and other repressed traditions and identities. Part of his project involved reversing the repression of the cultural minority identities that had been a prominent feature of Kemalist Turkish nationalism.

The new vision for Turkey became known as the Second Republic. The First Republic was created by Mustafa Kemal

Atatürk and was a break with the Ottoman past. The intellectual and political leaders of the Second Republic worked to demolish the repressive and militarized state structures of Kemalist Turkey and replace them with a new system of administration, civil control over the army, a free-market economy and liberal solutions to the Kurdish problem, as well as liberal policies concerning the cultural, ethnic and religious diversity of Turkey.

Özal's vision was a modern Turkish multiculturalism that did not reject the Ottoman past, but instead drew on the history of Turkey for inspiration, and his policies are sometimes referred to as neo-Ottomanism. This term often refers to a foreign policy vision that looks to the former lands of the Ottoman Empire, a large swathe of the Middle East and the Balkans, as Turkey's natural partners, but in Özal's ideology the Ottoman past also served as an important source of inspiration for the management of internal religious and ethnic diversity. The idea was to introduce a modern version of the Ottoman *millet* system in which religious and ethnic minorities enjoy autonomy and cultural rights.[12]

The liberal reforms Özal started created new opportunities for public expressions of Islam and a new religious civil society started to appear under and after his rule. Heightened religious participation is one of the effects of the new liberalization and the growth of religious civil society. Many of the formerly repressed minority groups appear in this new civil society as religious NGOs that aim to define and represent different versions of Islam for modern Turks within a societal sphere populated by a number of similar non-governmental religious organizations. One of these minority groups is the Alevis, a branch of Shia Islam influenced by Central Asian shamanism and with its own distinctive worship and rituals. Several Alevi NGOs are active in Turkey today promoting different visions for the establishment of an official and authentic form of Alevism.[13] This jockeying for a position of authority from which to define the real version of Alevism, or any other form of religion for that matter, is a typical consequence of government involvement in the market for religion.

The global Islamic movement of Fethullah Gülen is another important child of the more liberal Turkey. The Gülen movement espouses a tolerant Islam at ease with modern science and focused on education and enlightenment.[14] In today's Turkey, we can see many different consequences of the relaxing of state repression and the emergence of a religious civil society. One consequence that has been widely feared both in Turkey and in Western media was the rise of political Islam, or Islamism, after the partial relaxation of state repression of religious expressions outside of the official Turkish orthodoxy. The important consequence for my argument, however, is that Turkey has seen the growth of a new and liberal civil society, where the once-repressed Sufi networks can re-emerge as a strong social, and to some extent political, movement. It is reasonable to analyze this sector as a relatively free market for religion, at least far more free than it was between 1925 and 1950.

Turkey is a religious country in the sense that most Turks feel some kind of attachment to Islam and its doctrines, a high percentage of people pray and keep the fast during Ramadan. If this general demand for religion cannot be met by mainstream religion, such as the long-established Sufi networks that were so important for centuries of Ottoman rule, then other types of suppliers of religion will have more success in the market. From a market perspective, then, under state repression and monopoly we should expect more potential consumers of religion to look for alternative religious goods among groups that are outside the mainstream and specialize in avoiding the repression of the authorities. This is why it seems likely that a religious market with more freedom in today's Turkey has undermined support for radical religious groups.[15]

6

RELIGIOUS MARKETS IN HINDUISM

The first time I went to India I visited a large temple to the fierce goddess Kali in the city of Kolkata. One of the Brahmin priests in the temple asked me to take my shoes off, which is a natural thing to do when entering religious buildings. When I wanted to leave, he demanded a substantial sum of money to give me my shoes back. I consented grudgingly and have later come to realize that many religious specialists—not only Hindus, of course—have a talent for getting their hands on money. A number of less anecdotal and more scholarly examples could be offered to show that Hindu ritual sites and institutions are often about money and power, just like we find in Christianity or other religious traditions.

The Brahmins are the high caste people who define official and orthodox Hinduism. In the Hindu ideology expressed in legal texts written by Brahmins, a person's religious identity is linked to his or her position in the world of *dharma*. *Dharma* is the key concept of Indian social philosophy. It refers both to the natural order of the cosmos and the individual duties and privileges according to this order. There are three factors determining the position of an individual in this world. First, there is caste. Secondly, a person's current position in the ideal life-cycle defines a person's status in terms of age. Finally, there is gender. A person is born into a certain social category and moves through different stages from birth to death. On one level, religious identity is part of social and cultural identity.

The most famous of all Hindu texts, the Bhagavadgita, is a dialogue about *dharma* between the warrior Arjuna and God Krishna. Krishna explains to Arjuna that it is his duty as a warrior to fight bravely even though he has moral qualms about the impending battle. His duty, or his *dharma*, is determined by his caste and his stage of life. He is who he is because of his social position rather than individual choice. The same topic and the same conclusions can be found throughout the great epic Mahabharata, of which the Bhagavadgita is one small part. In fact, exactly the same perspectives are found throughout Hindu literature, particularly in the legal-religious books that were composed as guides to *dharma*. These texts are called *dharmasutras* and their goal is to explain the duties and privileges of the social classes. ("Social class" is a translation of the Sanskrit word "varna," which is not the same as caste, but is a hierarchical idea related to the caste system.)

Hierarchy or devotion?

Hinduism is strictly hierarchical in its social philosophy, with people's identities being defined by the social position into which they are born. From this perspective, religion looks deterministic and anti-individualistic. The market idea of religion looks utterly misplaced in this world of ascribed religious and social identities. But if we look more closely at the history of Hinduism, we realize that the idea of religion that we find in the authoritative texts about *dharma* is only one aspect of what actually went on in India through the centuries. Already in the fifth century BC, religious renouncers openly challenged and ridiculed the Brahminical idea about religious authority and identity. These renouncers insisted that salvation was in principle open to anybody with the right intellect and the stamina to study and practice meditation. One of these renouncers, Siddhartha, achieved the title Buddha, or the awakened. Both he and his disciples rejected the hierarchical social philosophy of the Brahmins and insisted that true religion was about achievement.

Buddhism eventually became a separate religion, but many of the revolutionary religious movements managed to stay within the bounds of orthodoxy and transformed Hinduism from within. Most important of all are the Hindu communities that make up what we call the *bhakti* movement. This movement of devotional religion, which first appeared in south India in the fifth and sixth centuries and was established in north India slightly later, centered on the personal relationship between devotee and deity. One fundamental characteristic of the *bhakti* movements was their separation of religious from social and cultural identities. In these movements, religion was a matter of choice and personal striving. Religious identity was about belonging to a group of like-minded people whose duties and privileges all accrued from their personal choices and abilities and not from their social position or from their cultural background.

The *bhakti* movements separated religious identity from social identity. In order to achieve membership of a religious community one had to undergo the ritual of initiation. This type of initiatory ritual was, however, not the right or privilege of a member of a social group like the life-cycle rituals of Brahminical society. In order to be accepted, an individual could in theory come from any class or caste. He or she had to be an adult suited for life in the community, but most importantly he or she had to wish to join the group and actively approach it. Religion became a matter of choice.

To women in particular, the separation of religious from social identity was very important because the *bhakti* movements often became a way to escape the severe restrictions placed on the social and religious life of women. In the devotional religion, which focused on the strong, personal, emotional bonds to a god, women could participate to the full despite their gender. Lower castes, too, often saw the devotional movements as possibilities to escape the degradation of everyday life in the village.

Tantrism was another movement that created religious identities transcending and relativizing caste and gender identities. In the seventh and eighth centuries, a new type of religious culture developed among Hindus, especially in Kashmir and Nepal in the north of the subcontinent and in Bengal in the east. This new culture was first found in groups devoted to the god Shiva, but it soon spread into other branches of Hinduism, and further into Buddhism and Jainism and even seeped into Islam at a later stage. The Tantric movement was a revolution against the conservative world of the Brahmins. A huge number of Tantric texts called Tantras were composed and the Tantric masters insisted that these were a far superior guide to real religion than the ancient Vedas. This view is in itself heretical from the orthodox Brahminical point of view. The Tantric masters and their disciples turned all the values of the Brahminical world on their head by engaging in very impure ritual practices involving meat-eating, alcohol consumption and sexual intercourse. Women were not seen as impure creatures but rather came to embody a special energy called *shakti*, which was absolutely necessary for religious realization.

So traditional Hindu religious identity was split into different types. On the one hand, an individual was born into a family, a hereditary profession, a caste and a class (*varna*), although the last category does not seem to have had a very great significance for non-Brahmins in everyday life despite its prominence in classical Sanskrit literature. With all these basic affiliations came a religious identity that was more or less taken for granted. On the other hand, throughout Indian history an individual could choose to undergo initiation into religious groups that were separate from the world of ascribed caste identities, like devotional *bhakti* groups or movements around a Tantric guru. Such membership was not ascribed by birth. It was achieved through initiation.

Through most of the history of Hinduism, an individual could have several distinct types of religious identity: first, one would have the communal or social religious identity defined by caste, which is expressed through everyday rituals and other behaviors, like restrictions on social contact with other groups. The key organizing principle of the caste system is purity. Lower castes harbor a religious type of impurity that can defile members of higher castes and many of the rules associated with caste can be understood as ways to avoid impurity. Secondly, many people would have a sectarian religious identity defined by the family's affiliation to a certain religious tradition and expressed through the devotion and rituals directed towards the sect's deity, and there was the option of a personal religion defined by one's chosen guru or saint, and expressed through devotion and obeisance to him. The different religious identities were bestowed by different types of people whose authority was limited to a defined sphere of religious life.

The important point is that Hinduism opened the door for very different types of religious identities and belonging long before meeting Western civilization. Only when we talk about the overarching identity based on caste is it right to say that Hindu religious identity is, and has always been, indistinguishable from social and cultural identity. The other types of religious belonging were always open to personal taste on the part of the consumer, and there was competition between suppliers. Hindu religious history provides many examples of this. A number of old Hindu texts show that Hinduism at many different points in history harbored a rich world of religious and philosophical teachers who were in stiff competition for followers. Sect leaders were often outspoken in their criticism of other religious groups and the stakes could be high in terms of number of followers and material wealth.

Hindu religious identities must be divided into several types or layers. On the one hand, there has always been the identity that is ascribed to people by birth. This is a social identity that comes with the caste and family of the newborn child and it is not possible to choose a different identity. This is who you are, if you are born a Hindu. If this communal or social identity were the only type of religious belonging that existed in pre-modern India, critics would be right in saying that there could never be religious markets in which religious goods could be offered by different teachers and groups and where consumers had a choice in where they wanted to turn for their religious consumption. Choice is not part of social identity in pre-modern Hinduism, but then again choice and mobility is not a big part of social identity in any pre-modern society. On the other hand, however, Hinduism has developed religious identities that are open to anybody and detached from the social religious identity associated with caste.

There has always been, then, a very important distinction between ascribed and achieved religious identities in India. The social identity that comes with caste is ascribed, while the religious identity associated with membership in a devotional movement is achieved. Achievement means that one has to ask to be taken up as a member and go through an initiation and some kind of learning process to be part of the group. The individual's own effort is what makes him or her into a member of the religious group. There is a choice in whether to apply for membership of this or that group, or simply stay out. This distinction between ascribed and achieved identities is of major importance in understanding how religion works in pre-modern and modern India because in the world of religious groups in which membership is achieved through individual effort we find competition, conversions, reconversions, switching between different groups and multiple types of religious identities. In other words, this is where we can look for religious markets.

The multi-religious marketplace

To realize how much of a religious marketplace pre-modern India often was, we also need to understand that the boundaries between what we now think of as different and compartmentalized religions were more fluid or less relevant in the everyday life of many Indians. In fact, the labels that modern historians use to analyze the past, words like Muslims, Hindus or Christians, have been unstable through time or simply have not been part of the vocabulary of the people we describe with these labels. Devotional cults often transcended religious boundaries. This was possible because many Indians had religious identities that were separated

105

from their social identities. They could be born as Hindu or Muslim, or as Sikh or Jain, and keep this ascribed communal identity throughout their life while also shopping around among saints and religious groups from different religions in their search for religious services. Such shopping around did not necessarily involve any conversion or loss of one's communal identity.

Muslim Sufi saints or Hindu sadhus, or indeed other holy men belonging to more or less well-defined traditions, would offer ways to get closer to God and to secure salvation. A saint would try to demonstrate that he had a good relationship with the divine, a sure way to convince customers of the quality of his goods, and the best way to show this would be to display magical powers. Many of the religious goods sought by the devotees of saints were closer to what we normally think of as magic. The saints would offer the help of their supernatural powers to grant worldly needs, like curing illness or achieving some material gain. On this point, there are clear parallels to Catholic tradition.

Kabir (1440–1518) was the most famous of the religious teachers who mixed devotional practices and ideas from Hinduism and Islam, as well as other traditions. He belonged to a large milieu of religious preachers, many of them itinerant, who competed for followers in north India. Kabir wrote religious poetry about the experience of God and mocked the ideas of religious authority and exclusivity held by all religious elites, like the Brahmins. Kabir's caste of weavers was Muslim, but that was just a formality as he rejected the authority of the Quran and Muslim intellectuals and elites, just as he rejected the authority of the holy Hindu texts, the Vedas. Folk traditions of Tantric yoga informed his religious practice along with Islamic Sufism and Hindu devotionalism. To Kabir, God, mostly addressed with the Hindu name Ram, was a loving, unfathomable and ineffable being. He called himself a child of both Rama and Allah and insisted that God was to be found everywhere, not only in the temple or the mosque.

This type of devotional religion became more important to the common people throughout much of India than the orthodox and elite conceptions of Brahminical Hinduism and Islam. It combined elements from Buddhism, which had by now almost disappeared from India, and from the great Hindu devotional movements, as well as from Sufism. In the northwestern part of the Indian subcontinent another important representative of this style of religion was born in 1469, just three decades after Kabir. He was Guru Nanak and would become the founder of Sikhism.

Let us look at a much less famous example of an environment where the power of saints was more relevant to the consumer of religion and magic than the labels of Hindu or Muslim. In the city of Aurangabad in the western Indian state of Maharashtra, we find a large shrine surrounding the tomb of the Sufi saint Shah Nur who died in 1692. At this time the Moghuls still ruled India, although the British had opened their trade at Kolkata in the east of the subcontinent. Muslims are a minority in Aurangabad and in Maharashtra in general and a large number of Shah Nur's devotees were Hindus.

The example of Shah Nur shows that the Hindu religious marketplace also included religious goods offered by Muslim saints. In fact, to people who lived in places like this, the labels of Hindu or Muslim would not be very important in their use of religious goods. In oral narratives about Shah Nur, the saint is described as a composite figure with traits that are drawn both from Muslim and Hindu sources.

Hindu and Muslim devotees would go to the saint who seemed most trustworthy, and where they rationally thought they would get most in return for their money and time, and some of the narratives available from Aurangabad describe competition for followers. A Hindu could keep his or her social caste identity while at the same time shopping around among Hindu sadhus and Muslim saints for religious goods. One scholar writes about the milieu around Shah Nur as a "saintly marketplace" where there was always a risk of followers choosing other saints because his powers seemed greater.[1]

What does this brief look at pre-modern India tell us about the relevance of an economic perspective on religion? Critics need to understand two important nuances in how religion has actually worked in India. First, there were several different layers or systems of religious identity. The communal or social identity that came with your caste was ascribed by birth. This is not the level at which the economic perspective is relevant because people did not see much choice in their communal identities. They could not switch caste or ethnic group as they wished, although there are examples of collective conversions of whole castes from Hinduism to Islam or Christianity.

However, the individual religious identities that people received by affiliating with holy men, like Muslim Sufi saints or Hindu sadhus, were a matter of choice. At this level of achieved religious identities there was certainly a marketplace for religious and magical goods in many parts of India throughout history. Hindus would visit the shrines of Muslim holy men. Muslims would visit the shrines of Hindu holy men. Worshippers were after religious goods and they were often free to approach the saint they thought supplied the best value for money.

Secondly, many of these religious marketplaces are not easily detectable if one simply reads the official historical texts written by Muslim intellectuals in Persian and Urdu, or by learned Hindus in Sanskrit and later in Hindi. The official stories of Indian religions often narrate how Islam or a certain branch of Hinduism was embraced by groups or individuals and how one religion was able to demonstrate its superiority over others. But such official histories are often ideologically biased views of the past, and the everyday reality for most Indians was often quite different.

7

RELIGIOUS MARKETS IN BUDDHISM

As a graduate student, I spent a lot of time reading some of the key texts of what is known as the Pali canon. These are the canonical texts of the branch of Buddhism called Theravada, which dominates in Thailand, Sri Lanka, Burma and Cambodia. I had the good fortune of studying under the supervision of a German professor who taught me Sanskrit and Pali and introduced me to these early Buddhist texts. One of the things that struck me about many of the texts of the Pali canon was the fact that the environment of the Buddha was generally presented as a market for religious and philosophical ideas.

There are three characteristics of this environment that I take to constitute a market for religion: plurality, competition and political neutrality towards the religious firms. Many of the early Buddhist texts present us with an environment at the time of the Buddha where there were a large number of religious groups or organizations. These groups were led by people who offered particular philosophical worldviews and programs for religious practice. There was fierce competition between these groups for members or adherents and for the status and material wealth that came with a large following. Many of the dialogues of the Buddha,

111

which are recorded in texts called *suttas*, are about the competition between the Buddha and other religious leader of the day. It is not surprising to find that the Buddha always wins these competitions since the texts we are looking at are biased in favor of Buddhism. They are after all Buddhist texts. But the important point is that they all portray competition as rhetorical fights in which there is no external political force that tips the scales, but where the power of the arguments decide.

When I first read these texts, I never got around to writing down my thoughts about the market for religion. Instead, I wrote a book about the picture of the psychology of conversion appearing from the same texts.[1] One of the pleasures in writing the present book is to be able to return to some of those texts and their world and explore this ancient example of an environment that comes quite close to an ideal free market for religion.

Let me mention some examples. The *suttas*, as I mentioned, are very early texts recording the dialogues and debates of the Buddha. In a text called the Samannaphala Sutta (The *sutta* about the fruits of the life as a recluse), we meet a king by the name of Ajatasattu. He was king of Magadha, a large state that came into existence during the Buddha's lifetime by incorporating several smaller republics. This *sutta* starts with the king sitting on his palace's terrace roof in the middle of the night under the full moon, surrounded by his ministers. He is restless and needs someone to talk to. In fact, he is more than restless: he is tormented by the fact that he has killed his own father to gain power. The Buddha, who is a wandering ascetic traveling between the cities of the area, happens to be in the vicinity. The king asks his ministers if there is anybody among the philosophers and ascetics who could give a talk worth listening to. One of the ministers then replies:

> There is, Sire, Purana Kassapa, the head of an order, of a following, the teacher of a school, well known and of repute as a sophist, revered by the people, a man of experience, who has long been a recluse, old and well stricken in years. Let your Majesty pay a visit to him. It may well be that, on calling upon him, your heart, Sire, shall find peace.[2]

Ajatasattu does not answer, so the other ministers suggest other teachers that the king might want to visit and talk to. Altogether, six famous and respected leaders of different schools and orders are presented as potential dialogue partners, but the king is not convinced as he has already spoken to them and was not impressed by their answers. Finally, his physician suggests that he go to see the Buddha—he might have some enlightening thoughts to share with the sleepless monarch. The king sets out on his elephant with a retinue of followers and reaches the Buddha and his large crowd of monks. He bows respectfully to the Buddha and sits down beside him. He then asks if he can tell him about any immediate, visible fruits of the life of the recluse. The Buddha will answer, but first he wants to know if the king has talked to other teachers about the same issue. The king explains that he has in fact seen the six teachers his ministers suggested earlier in the evening and he relates to the Buddha how they presented their teachings. The king says that he was unhappy with the answers they gave, but did not want to offend them by expressing any dissatisfaction, so on all previous occasions he neither accepted nor rejected their viewpoints but departed as soon as it was polite to do so. After long debates, the Samannaphala Sutta ends with King Ajatasattu begging the Buddha to take him into his order as a monk.

Texts like the Samannaphala Sutta present a social environment in northern India at the time of the Buddha with a mind-boggling plurality of religious leaders and schools with widely different worldviews and teachings. Some wear strange clothes, some walk around naked. Some live in the wilderness, some stay in the towns. Some preach deterministic doctrines of karma and retribution, while others preach nihilistic and materialistic atheism. The wielders of political power treat all these recluses with respect and there seems to be no alliance between the state and any particular religious organization. From the evidence of these texts, it is reasonable to say that there existed a competitive market for religion at the time of the Buddha.

The famous Buddhist text called *The Questions of King Milinda* starts with a description of the city of Sagala in the land of the Yonakas. Yonaka means Ionian and refers to the Greek empire of Bactria, in today's Afghanistan. King Milinda was a Greek king, and in the text that bears his name his city is described in detail as a center of trade. There are shops selling luxury goods of every kind. You can get the most refined silks and jewelry, and sweet odors of flowers and perfumes flow from the bazaars. The city is full of money, gold and silver, and its streets and marketplaces are bustling with animals and people of every walk of life. Religious teachers are a natural part of this activity. In the words of the text, "The streets resound with cries of welcome to the teacher of every creed, and the city is the resort of the leading men of each of the differing sects."[3] The presence of the religious teachers is an aspect of the city's bustling trade.

The text tells the story of how King Milinda wanted to discuss philosophy with somebody who could challenge his own views about the world, and his advisers tell him that he might see some of the six famous teachers of the area, but after asking them questions he realizes that they are not able to satisfy his religious curiosity and he continues to look for somebody wiser until he ends up in the company of the Buddhist monk Nagasena. Buddhist literature has many other examples of kings and nobles shopping around for answers to existential problems. As they are Buddhist texts, the protagonists usually choose the solution of the Lord Buddha to the answers of other philosophers, but this does not change the strong impression that we are looking at a free market for religion. Kings, rich traders and more humble householders of the towns are all portrayed in this literature as consumers of the religious or philosophical services that are offered by a broad range of different teachers and the movements they lead. These teachers are entrepreneurs who devote their lives to founding schools of religious and philosophical ideas and meditational practice. Some of these schools survived, but most did not.

What religious goods does Buddhism offer?

If we are going to adjust the religious economies model to the Buddhist world, we need to pay attention to the real differences between the nature of religion in societies that are dominated by the Abrahamic creeds, on the one hand, and Buddhist societies on the other. Much of the research about religious economies in the Christian world sees salvation after death as the ultimate product offered by Christian churches. But what exactly has Buddhism to offer its consumers? Why have people chosen to pay for its products to the extent that Buddhism has become a world religion with half a billion followers and considerable wealth and privileges in many societies?

On the highest level, of course, Buddhism does offer salvation, although this looks very different from salvation in a traditional Christian or Muslim sense. Buddhism has nirvana, which is the complete cessation of all the mental and physical forces that produce new existence, new rebirths and renewed suffering. In a strict sense, one could say that the Buddha offered to the world only insight, deep knowledge, about the exact nature of human existence and the forces that keep us striving for safety, for material goods, for social belonging and the other things that keep us tied to existence. He also offered a way—the holy eightfold path—that would lead out of this trap and end in the cessation of rebirth and in nirvana. Armed with this insight—neatly summed up in the four noble truths—any human being could in theory reach nirvana. The only problem is that this insight and the practice it requires are exceedingly difficult. It requires not only intelligence but also enormous personal effort and a willingness to forsake the comforts of normal life. Most Buddhist schools and teachers would say that it is impossible to reach nirvana while leading a normal life with a family and a job. You need to become a monk or nun, and even then it is hard. No wonder, then, that for most Buddhists, the product that had any relevance was not about real salvation—not about nirvana at all—but rather about how to make sure that one's next rebirth was as comfortable as possible.

The product that really appealed to people throughout Buddhist history was good karma. Or rather, it was the result of good karma (i.e. religious merit), which in Sanskrit was called *punya*. "Karma" simply means action, and Buddhist worldviews throughout Asia have always built on the basic idea that all living beings are reborn and their actions in this life have consequences for their future existence. If you do something nasty to somebody, you will most likely experience unpleasant consequences in your next life, but if you do good deeds, you will reap benefits. If you have been really good, you may hope to be reborn as a human being and lead a pleasant life. One of the good things about being born as a human being is the ability to understand the truth of Buddhist doctrine. There is nothing deterministic about this, according to Buddhist teachings, and there is always a possibility to nudge one's future wellbeing in a positive direction by being nice.

In many Buddhist societies, people have also believed that religious merit can be transferred to other people, like dead family members, and used to increase their chances of a good rebirth, although this idea is not really part of official Buddhist teachings in any school, as far as I know. The third broad range of products that Buddhism has offered is simply magic. Just like other universal and missionary religions, official Buddhism has frowned on folk religion and magical practices, but in the real world this was very important to Buddhists. Buddhist monks and texts would offer ways to cure a range of diseases, ways to avoid snakebite, or magical chants to charm a man or woman into your arms.

So Buddhism has always offered at least two rather different products—nirvana and religious merit—that are different from the products offered by Christian churches. In certain ways, Buddhist worldviews are actually better adapted to facilitate the exchange of goods and payment between producers and consumers than those of Christianity.

According to Buddhism, however, it was part of the basic teachings that paying land, food, buildings and other material goods to the monks and nuns and to their monasteries would buy religious merit that could be used to secure a favorable rebirth. Actually, the word buy is technically incorrect because the religious merit was not something that the monks and nuns actually had in store and could give away; it was rather an effect that was produced more or less mechanically by the exchange. Nevertheless, this was the exchange that was the pivot of the whole religious economy of Buddhist societies from the time of the Buddha up until today.

Ashoka and the beginnings of religious monopoly

We cannot be certain about the dates of the Buddha, but it is probably about right to say that he died around 400 BC. Over the next century, Buddhism spread out to many parts of India and soon its missionaries started moving beyond the subcontinent, to places like Kashmir, Burma and Sri Lanka. The Buddha urged his monks to proselytize. In a famous text he is recorded as asking them to travel out in all directions and preach in local languages that people could understand. He had little but contempt for the orthodox Brahmanical ideas about holy language that restricted access to the philosophical and ritual treasures of Hinduism.

Under Emperor Ashoka, Buddhism entered a new and decisive phase in its early history. Ashoka became emperor in the Maurya dynasty around 270 BC. He was the most important ruler of pre-Islamic India—his empire covered almost all of what is today India and much of Pakistan. To modern India, he represents the glorious past of the nation and his symbols are everywhere. The state symbol of the Republic of India is the lion capital of Ashoka found at Sarnath. The lion capital is a representation of four lions standing back to back on an abacus. Originally, lion capitals were placed on top of tall, smooth pillars of stone that

Ashoka raised in different locations in his empire. These pillars are covered with inscriptions in which the emperor gives information or instructions. Together with similar inscriptions carved into rocks they provide us with invaluable clues to the political and cultural history of ancient India. Sculptors always placed a large stone wheel on top of the lions of the lion capitals. The wheel is highly significant. But what exactly does it mean?

The wheel is a symbol of *dharma*, which simply means the teaching of the Buddha. Ashoka was a Buddhist. But it is more complicated than that because the emperor seems to have made an interesting distinction between his own religious affiliation, on the one hand, and his public announcement about morality and justice, on the other. If we read his inscriptions carefully, we will see that they can be categorized in several ways. There is a big difference between the strikingly beautiful stone pillars with lion capitals and the cruder major and minor inscriptions made in rocks. There is also a difference in the contents of the messages inscribed by the emperor to the general population and those of the messages inscribed for the benefit of the Buddhist Sangha, i.e. the order of monks and nuns.

For instance, in a minor rock inscription at a place called Bhabra, Ashoka's message was addressed directly to the monks. "You know, Sirs," the emperor says, "how deep is my respect for and faith in the Buddha, the Dhamma and the Sangha." Then he instructs the monks and nuns about exactly what texts they should recite to themselves and to laypeople in order to ensure the long survival of Buddhism. In another minor rock inscription, he announces that he has traveled to the village of Lumbini, the place where the Buddha was born, and raised a stone pillar and given the town exemption from taxes. In an inscription called the Schism Edict, which has been found in the same version in several places in north India, Ashoka addresses the monks and nuns about internal order and cohesion in the Sangha. No one is to cause dissent in the order, the emperor insists. The Sangha of monks and nuns has been united and it should stay united as long as the sun and the moon last. Whoever causes a schism in the order is to be put in white garments and taken out of the community of monks and nuns. In the same edict, Ashoka orders that a copy of the text must be kept in the meeting hall of the Sangha and another copy must be given to the laity. The texts must be circulated and made known. He also insists that laypeople must come to the Sangha on *uposatha* days (i.e. particular days of the month when the formal and constitutive ritual of the Sangha is performed). Since there was no central authority in the Buddhist order, every self-sufficient community of monks and nuns must hold their own rituals in order to continue to be a real Buddhist Sangha. So when Ashoka warns against schisms, the warning is probably to be interpreted as a warning directed at a number of individual Sanghas and their monasteries, and not at some abstract notion of the Buddhist Church.

Ashoka is of great significance for our investigation of the religious market in early Buddhism. This was the first time that a ruler had intervened directly in the internal legal and doctrinal affairs of the Sangha. Up to this point, Buddhist monks had certainly worked hard to get support from kings and rich merchants, but in Ashoka they had a ruler who not only facilitated competition among the different religious groups but also wanted to regulate them and make sure they behaved properly and did not succumb to internal conflicts and factionalism. In edicts addressed to the population in general, rather than to the monks and nuns, the emperor explains how he has created a new class of bureaucrats to oversee affairs of *dharma*. They are called *dharma-mahama-tras* in the language of the edicts, which can be translated as morality officials. So when he addressed his people as the universal emperor, and not as a pious Buddhist, the word *dharma* took on a subtle change in meaning. In these public inscriptions, it no longer referred specifically to the Buddhist *dharma* (i.e. the teaching of the Buddha), but instead pointed to a highly abstract concept of morality and just living that everybody could adhere to regardless of their religious affiliation.

I have no need to add to the praise that has been showered on Ashoka for being the first defender of human rights and freedom of belief—such things seem somewhat anachronistic to me. However, it is difficult not to be impressed by Ashoka's use of the concept of *dharma* to promote a civil religion that could unite the diverse peoples inhabiting a truly multicultural empire. An important way to follow the morality of *dharma*, according to Ashoka, was to support different kinds of religious groups with donations. Even though Ashoka himself was a Buddhist, he wanted people to be engaged in the field of religion in general and he was happy if they adhered to one of the other groups, like Jainism or Ajivikism.

We can compare the situation of Buddhism during its two first centuries with the plight of Christianity in the early Roman Empire. The fate of the early Christians depended to a large degree on the emperor who happened to be in office. Some emperors tolerated Christians, while others persecuted them, as I discussed in an earlier chapter. But the situation changed dramatically under Constantine the Great in the early fourth century, and from that time onwards Christianity's marriage to political power would secure its future as a religious monopoly in Europe. The fate of Buddhism, however, was not secure after Ashoka because soon Hindu kings would establish a new empire in which Buddhism was seen to be a threat to orthodox Brahmanical Hinduism.

Tibet's state church

There is something magical about traveling north from the steaming hot and densely populated plains of northern India. The towns and cities along the Ganges and its tributaries were teeming with people and activity already at the time of the Buddha and it is quite possible to imagine what it must have been like 2,500 years ago. When your car or bus moves north, things change. Soon the air is cooler, your vehicle struggles with winding roads, and, then, in the distance you see the snow-capped peaks of the Himalayas.

In significant ways, the axis between the plains of India and the mountains to the north was the most important connection in the cultural history of Asia. The Buddha himself came from a little kingdom on the slopes of the mountains on the border between today's Nepal and India, but he knew that he had to travel down to the larger cities on the Indian plains to win the support and following he wanted. India was the home of his teaching for 1,500 years after his death, but when Turkish conquerors pressed down from Afghanistan and towards the eastern regions of north India in the eleventh and twelfth centuries AD, Buddhism started losing the status it had enjoyed for centuries. At the end of the twelfth century, a Turkish general destroyed the great Buddhist university of Nalanda and set fire to its immense library with its treasures of manuscripts. Monks were killed and their monasteries were destroyed. From this time onwards, Islam would be the favored religious culture supported by north Indian rulers. It is certainly true that a wide variety of Hinduism would continue to be practiced and tolerated and often blended with Islam into devotional folk-religion, but Buddhism struggled to keep afloat. We do not know exactly why. There may have been several reasons, but I suspect it had become too elitist and lacked a broad basis among common people.

This could easily have been the beginning of the end for the tradition of Mahayana[4] Buddhist philosophy that had flourished after the sophisticated philosophical treatises composed by Nagarjuna as far back as the second and third centuries AD. However, history took a course that would shape Buddhism in new ways. The great Buddhist teachers of northern India traveled north to the mountains. They struggled through the mountain passes of the Himalayas and reached Tibet. As the new Turkish masters of India took little interest in the mountains, they proved a perfect field for Buddhist missionary activity. Buddhism was not new to Tibet. Tibetan kings of the seventh and eighth centuries had supported Buddhism, but the Tibetan empire collapsed in the middle of the ninth century and descended into civil wars and political fragmentation, which effectively ended state support for any religious group.

During the twelfth and thirteenth centuries, a great deal of plurality developed in Tibetan Buddhism with intense competition between four main schools. There was also some competition from the religious tradition called Bon, which seems to have been an indigenous religious culture predating Buddhism that contained strong shamanistic elements. This environment, with no strong political power backing a religious monopolist and with a continuing influx of Buddhist teachers and their ideas from India, amounted to a relatively free market for religion in Tibet. The stakes were high because the Buddhist schools of Tibet competed for a range of resources: land, riches, food, people and political power. In this environment, a charismatic monk called Tsongkhapa (1357–1419) founded the Geluk school of Buddhism and started building what was to become Tibet's state religion.[5]

The Geluk school, or the Yellow Hats as it is often called, was doctrinally not fundamentally different from the other Buddhist schools when it was founded. They all read the works by Nagarjuna and the famous commentators on his Mahayana philosophy called the Madhyamaka (The middle way). However, the Geluk school sought to gain a competitive advantage by some key innovations. They specialized in mass monasticism and only accepted ordained abbots, not lay abbots, and they were strict on discipline. The focus on developing monastic culture made the Geluk school less reliant on clan politics than the other schools and this seems to have been a precondition for future growth in monks, monasteries and power. The Geluk school also created a system of monastic organization in which the head abbot of the main Geluk monastery (the Ganden monastery) is the highest leader of the school.

They also established the lineage of the Dalai Lama, who is the incarnation of the bodhisattva of compassion, Avalokiteshvara, and the Panchen Lama who is the incarnation of the Buddha Amitabha. The institution of these highly esteemed Lamas has been crucial to the Geluk school's success. In the mid-sixteenth century, the learned fifth Dalai Lama unified central Tibet after a period of war and established himself as both political and religious head of Tibet. Seeing the present Dalai Lama's smiling face in the news it is easy to forget that he is the leader of a religious school that spent much of its energy from the 1500s on capturing a promising religious market by forging alliances with Mongol khans and fighting wars with other Buddhist schools. The gains from winning this contest included control over substantial economic resources and great political power. In modern times, the Geluk is the state religion of Tibet and has played an important role as a symbol of Tibetan national identity and resistance in the period following the Chinese occupation in 1959.

State religion in Sri Lanka, Thailand and Burma

It is a commonplace among scholars to say that Buddhism was the established religion, the state religion, of Sri Lanka from the conversion of King Devanampiya Tissa in the third century BC. There is no doubt that Buddhism played an enormously important role in the culture of the people who inhabited Sri Lanka from this period, including the king and his family, but the big problem, often overlooked, is the same as the one we noted when we looked at Ashoka. The state was not a state in any modern and recognized sense of the word. The early Sinhalese kings had their capital in Anuradhapura in the northern dry zone of the island and their military power and their ability to exact taxes were necessarily limited not only by the technological and administrative limitations of the time but also by the very considerable political instabilities that were a fact of life in the following centuries.

The most important documents of early Sri Lanka, chronicles written in Pali and documenting the wars of kings and their relations to the Sangha, depict a situation where Buddhist institutions enjoyed a very close connection with political power and were a defining feature of Sinhalese identity. This seems to have been strengthened by the fact that several of the most important kings were forced to fight defensive wars against invading armies that came across the sea from the Indian mainland.

In medieval Sri Lanka, a series of reforms integrated the Sangha more closely into the state. The Buddhist King Parakramabahu I (1153–86) carried out a reform of Buddhism and enacted a new law code for the monks. The law code was written down by the leading monk of the time, but it is significant that it was the king who enacted it by royal order. Slightly later, King Parakramabahu II (1236–71) issued a document that gives details about how the Sangha should be organized. The principles of organization remained more or less intact until the Sinhalese state and its economy started to unravel in the sixteenth century, partly as a result of the arrival of European colonial powers, beginning with the Portuguese in the early 1500s. Since Sri Lanka was seen to be the model Theravada Buddhist country, the Buddhist states of Southeast Asia, like Thailand, adopted the same organizational principles and structures. To simplify a little, we can say that a highly hierarchical structure came into being from as early as the thirteenth century in which the Buddhist "church" was integrated in the framework of the state and where the high officials of the monkhood got their ultimate authority from those who held political power. At the same time, the Sangha and its symbols were important in creating religious legitimacy for the king and his rule. The monks were in charge of the Holy Tooth Relic and the ritual life surrounding it, and no Sinhalese king could claim legitimate power without the possession of this crucial religious and political symbol. For many centuries, the chief monk (the Sangharaja, i.e. "king of the Sangha") and other high religious officials have been appointed by the king. By communicating with and controlling the Sangharaja, the king had some leverage over the internal affairs of the monkhood.

In modern Thailand, the highest institutional authority in the Sangha is in the hands of the Council of Elders. This is a group of thirteen senior monks who are chosen by the Department of Buddhist Affairs and officially appointed by the king. The foremost among the thirteen is appointed to be the Sangharaja. Both of the two largest sects of Thai Buddhism—the Maha Nikaya and the Dhammayut—are equally represented in the Council of Elders and the office of Sangharaja alternates between the two despite the fact that the Mahanikaya is much larger than the Dhammayut. This way of running the affairs of the Sangha shows how Buddhism in modern times has been both subjugated by the secular power and highly centralized in a way unimaginable before the eighteenth century when these trends started. The administrative structure of the Buddhist Sangha in Thailand has several more layers of offices and we need not go into the details and functions of each of them here. The important fact is that the Department of Buddhist Affairs, and ultimately the king, has the power to appoint monks in all the offices of power.

8

RELIGIOUS MARKETS IN
MEDIEVAL CATHOLICISM

The most successful business venture in world history is probably the Catholic Church. Its organization developed gradually and underwent many transitions during its first centuries. Around 540, St Benedict (*c*.480–550), drawing on earlier monastic principles and values expressed in the writings of St Augustine and other early Christian thinkers, created his detailed and precise directory of the spiritual and administrative life of the Catholic monastery. The Rule of St Benedict soon became the code for the organization of the life of monks throughout Western Europe. The Benedictine monks formed the backbone of Catholic Christianity, and from the eighth to the twelfth centuries Benedictine monasticism was by far the most important form of religious life in Western Christendom. In 1098, a group of Benedictine monks established the Cistercian order at Cîteaux in the French region of Burgundy because they believed the Rule of St Benedict was not followed in the strict way it was meant to. The Cistercians had great success and their monasteries soon dominated the religious market both in France and the British Isles.

Both the original Benedictine and the new Cistercian monasteries formed an efficient network of firms that operated as what economists today would call franchise monopolists. If you want to know what a franchise looks like, think of McDonald's. Most McDonald's restaurants are not run by the company itself but through franchise agreements. This means that a local operator obtains the rights to use the McDonald's logo and its business model and to sell its hamburgers and fries. In return, the operator, called the franchisee, pays McDonald's, called the franchisor, a fee based on sales.

The medieval Benedictine or Cistercian monastery formed relationships to the Church and its central management in Rome that looked a bit like the relationship between the typical local McDonald's restaurant and the company headquarters in the United States. True, the nature of the products on sale is different—but not that different. The key characteristic of the product of the Church is not that it is related to death and what happens after, but that it is an intangible good where the customer lacks good information about quality. Hamburgers are far more concrete: once you bite into one, you know what it tastes like. (I am both too snobbish and too vegetarian to ever set foot in a McDonald's, by the way.)

In the buying and selling of certain kinds of goods, like eternal salvation, some forms of modern medical treatment, or car maintenance, the customer has very limited insight into the actual quality and efficiency of the good he or she is buying. There is an expert at the other end—a priest, a doctor or a car mechanic—telling you what is wrong with your soul, your body or your car, and also what type of treatment you need to get it right. You cannot really check the expert's diagnosis unless you happen to be an expert yourself. We call such goods credence goods; they are about the credibility of the retailer and the trust of the customer. In goods where there is this kind of asymmetry of information, where the customer cannot really experience the quality of the good, there are obvious incentives for fraud. The priest (or the doctor or the car mechanic) may sell you a lousy product without you ever finding out.

So the medieval monasteries sold a good that we can call assurance of salvation for the sake of simplicity, and the monks relied on the strong brand name provided by the pope in their local marketing. There was no big, yellow "M," but a lot of big crosses and other trusted symbols. The pope and his Curia, which is the papal court with all its functionaries residing in Rome, guaranteed the theological foundation of the goods offered by the monasteries. The business gradually became vertically integrated in the sense that the pope and his court, in their role as manufacturer and franchisor of salvation, tried to control the retail end of their product in several ways. They entered into contracts with individual monasteries and their abbots and created auditing and visitation systems to check that the retail end of the salvation business worked the way they wanted.[1]

The franchise model of the Catholic Church was present to varying degrees through the Middle Ages, but prior to the settlement of the Investiture Controversy at the Concordat of Worms in 1122 centralized control was complicated by the fact that lay rulers, including the Holy Roman emperor, wanted to have a say in the nomination of bishops and lower clerics. In the ninth and tenth centuries, the conflict between religious and secular authorities was often intense, but with the Concordat of Worms in 1122, the conflict was settled to the pope's advantage. From now on, the Church had complete control over its own organization and could expand and consolidate its business model throughout most of Western Europe.

The right price of salvation

In much of the Middle Ages, the Catholic Church enjoyed a monopoly in religious goods. The Church had no real competitors. Now and then heretical movements arose claiming that they could provide better salvation at a lower price, but these movements were mostly dealt with by violence or coercion. From the eleventh century, heresy became more widespread and in the following centuries the Church spent much energy on stamping out these threats to its monopoly position.

In the twelfth century, the Church developed the doctrine of purgatory, a major innovation. In early Christianity, believers looked at two possible fates after death: heaven or hell. Purgatory was a third mode of existence, a state of temporal punishment between this life and the final destination. It was a place or condition in which venial sins committed in life could be burnt away to make the soul ready for heaven. Purgatory has an extremely slim basis in the Bible, but the idea of a temporal state of a purifying pain after death is found in the writings of several early Church Fathers, among them St Augustin. It also seems to be logically implied in the Catholic traditions for prayer for the dead, but was only made an official doctrine of the Catholic Church at the Second Council of Lyon in 1274. The most colorful treatment of the expiating pains of purgatory was offered by the greatest of medieval poets, Dante Alighieri, in his *Divine Comedy*, which was finished just before he died in 1321.

The new doctrine was coupled with the practice of indulgences. The Catholic Church taught that Christ had bestowed on the Church the right to manage a treasury of his infinite merit. Christ's infinite merit was available to the Church and this could be used by priests to guarantee early release from the torments of purgatory against payment.[2] Release time from purgatory was the best business idea in the Western world between the thirteenth and the fifteenth century and provided the foundation for the immense profits netted by the Catholic Church during the later Middle Ages.

Imagine for a moment that salvation could be tailor-made and sold to individual customers at the highest price they were able and willing to pay. Any sensible business firm will try to sell its goods at the highest profit possible and would love to know the exact demand curve of each customer. If you have been very naughty and happen to have a high income, in finance say, we can offer salvation for US$10,000. If you are a professor with a modest income, like me, and have behaved impeccably, the price is far more reasonable. In many areas of Europe, priests had very good knowledge of the local communities in which they sold their goods and they would often know in detail the assets and income of individual laypersons. The Church used systems of tier pricing according to which rich people would pay a high price and poor people would pay far less. Often these systems were elaborate with a large number of tiers and individualized pricing mechanisms according to the means of the customer.[3]

If a local retailer working as franchisee can set the price at his own discretion, there is a danger that he restricts sales and increases the price of each unit sold in order to increase profit. There is also the opposite danger, that he reduces prices to a minimum and sells goods that are of low quality. In order to counter these risks, the producer of the good will state in the contract that the franchiser must sell the goods at a price between a lower floor and an upper ceiling. In the case of the pope and the monasteries, the price floor and price ceilings were fixed in confession manuals. These texts set a lower and upper price limit for each type of sin committed.

Maximizing profits by stimulating competition

Release time from purgatory was invented as a new religious product in Christian Europe in the middle of the thirteenth century and this went hand in hand with far-reaching organizational innovations. The Church is based on territorial divisions. The basic administrative unit of Christianity was and is the diocese governed by a bishop and divided into parishes governed by a parish priest, or the pastor.

Medieval monasteries and their priests acting as franchisees and retailers of salvation had exclusive rights to sell their product within a specific area. This is typical of franchise business models and ensures that local operations do not interfere in each other's sales. We could mention that the monasteries had many other lines of business, depending on the region, like the production of wool or wine, for instance, but such industry is not of immediate interest to our investigation of the Church as a monopolist of religious products.

Inside its territory, typically a parish, a monastery and its leadership enjoyed a local monopoly situation with all the familiar temptations to make life easier for themselves by selling goods and services of lower quality, in lesser quantities and at higher prices. The potential laziness on the part of the local retailer was a threat to the Church because it would seriously diminish the revenues sent back to Rome. The pope could perhaps have designed a system of competition between local parishes, but with the limitations on information gathering and control characteristic of the age it would seem a much better idea to introduce stiff and committed competition from outside.

A solution was offered in the orders of friars that were established in the period. In the early thirteenth century, St Dominic and St Francis established orders of friars and a number of mendicant groups were united as the Augustinians. All these orders were devoted to preaching and a life in poverty. Many friars were learned and traveled widely—they would become key to the spreading of Christianity outside Europe from the sixteenth century. In earlier times, the Church in Rome was often suspicious of mendicants who placed themselves outside the existing organization of the Church because their work implied a critique of the old ways, but under Innocent III, who was pope from 1198 to 1216, the orders of friars got their papal stamp of approval and were granted the right to preach and sell indulgences unrestricted by parochial borders. The orders of friars were not started with this intention in mind, but soon they were integrated in the formal organization of the Church.

The entry of the orders of Franciscans, Dominicans and Augustinians introduced a new kind of competition between two different types of suppliers: on one side, the local and traditional; on the other side, the new and mobile. The establishment of the orders of friars had the important consequence of introducing competition into the medieval business of salvation—as if the company headquarters of McDonald's decided that their franchise stores did not work hard enough to sell burgers and came up with the idea of mobile McDonald's vans manned by particularly committed and highly trained staff who could roam around at will and offer the perfect Big Mac at the right price. The new friars traveled the towns and cities in their black or brown cloaks and sold release time from purgatory, while the parish priests and old monasteries were often fiercely opposed to such practices and saw them as a threat to the bonds between the local religious establishment and its flock.

Capitalism and crusades

There were many reasons behind the increasing importance of the doctrine of purgatory and the institution of indulgences, and I am only focusing on the part of the picture that is relevant to my analysis of the Catholic Church as a firm in a marketplace for religion. In the thirteenth and fourteenth centuries, as we are approaching the seismic shifts of the Reformation, the Church still enjoyed the monopoly it had secured over some centuries, but at the same time sought ways to bind laypeople more tightly to the Church and develop religious goods that were attractive enough to prevent them from turning to the heresies that popped up in some parts of Europe. In other words, the threat from increasing religious diversity was probably one of the reasons for the doctrinal and organizational innovations in the Catholic Church that we have looked at here.

The demand for indulgences, which made the concept such an economic success, was also clearly connected to the rise of new economic classes. Usury was forbidden in ecclesiastical law, and people who engaged in this business were condemned to hell. The relationship between precept and practice being what it is in human culture—certainly not straightforward and simple—these laws did not prevent moneylenders from going about their business, but they certainly created fertile soil for religious ideas and services that would solve the tension and dissonance between the worldly need to make a living and the prospects of eternal damnation.

In the new doctrine of purgatory, usurers got a solution to their plight. Salvation became a matter of paying—it was monetarized. They could go on lending money, they could train their sons in the business, with the comforting knowledge that the sins they committed at work could be burnt off and expiated in purgatory, so that entry to heaven could be expected in the end. In this way, the doctrine of purgatory eased the burdens of growing communities of moneylenders in late medieval Europe, and therefore, the invention of purgatory in the twelfth century and its official recognition in the thirteenth century may have been essential in laying the foundations for modern capitalism.[4] This idea is contrary to the famous theory of Max Weber about the Protestant roots of modern capitalism, but it follows Weber in its focus on the historical and economic weight of religious doctrine.

Part of the reason behind the success of purgatory must also be sought in the fight that Christian Europe started with the Islamic world. The crusades were deeply religious undertakings and always contained an important element of penitence. In several English prayers from the thirteenth century there is a very explicit parallel between the purgatorial suffering of individual souls and the suffering of the Holy Land under Muslim rule. In these prayers, priests and congregations ask God to free the soul of a certain individuals, a family member for instance, from their torments in purgatory, and in the next sentence ask him to help the crusaders to free the Land that God's Son dedicated with his blood from the hands of infidel enemies.[5]

Markets across cultures

What is the use of looking at Islam, medieval Hinduism, early Buddhism or the medieval Catholic Church from an economic perspective? Religion poses a serious political problem in most parts of the world today and we badly need to take a fresh look at the relationship between government and faith. Economic theory offers concepts and tools for such a fresh look. Perhaps we can cut the Gordian knot of religion and politics by treating religious organizations like firms selling goods and services. This perspective may also take away some of the fear, awe and suspicion that often poison how we talk about and treat religion. Religions offer stuff that people want to pay for. Religions should be allowed to operate in markets regulated in a way that promotes freedom, fairness and equality.

The point I have been making in the last four chapters is that the economic and social scientific study of religion has made a mistake in confining the market analysis of religion to the modern, Christian West. In Islam, in Hinduism, in Buddhism and in Catholic Christianity there have existed several systems or layers of religious identities. On the most basic level, social-religious identities have often been immutable and ascribed by birth. But at the same time, inside these highly diverse civilizations there have always existed religious cultures and movements—and individual shaykhs, gurus, monks and ascetics—that have been more or less open and available to individuals regardless of ascribed identities and social status. People have been able to choose achieved religious identities, like membership in a Sufi order or a Hindu *bhakti* group or a Buddhist order of nuns. They have been able to consume the religious products offered by the groups and its leadership and there has often been competition between groups and leaders. All these groups and leaders have contributed to the creation of more or less regulated markets for supply and consumption of religious goods and services. I am not saying that free markets for religion have always existed everywhere. There have certainly been many historical situations where jealous monopolistic religious groups have colluded with brutal governments to stamp out all alternatives. I am saying, however, that markets for religion have in fact existed in numerous periods in many different cultures and civilizations. Therefore, the market perspective is relevant across cultures and through history.

To illustrate the continuum between achieved and ascribed religious identities, let us for a moment imagine three different people. The first one is the Jewish Canadian singer and poet Leonard Cohen, the second is a Muslim woman I know called Ayesha living in Birmingham and the third one is a fictional woman called Deepa living some-where in India in the early seventeenth century. Leonard Cohen was born a Jew and has become a Buddhist monk. He has an ascribed identity as a Jew and an achieved identity as a Buddhist at the same time. This is a common phenom-enon. Ayesha had an ascribed identity as Muslim from birth, but from living in a highly diverse society she became gradu-ally more aware of her religious identity as she grew into adulthood and started taking it less for granted. When she was twenty-five, her Muslim identity was something she actively chose to embrace. So in Ayesha's case we meet a woman who has a Muslim identity through life, but the nature of this religious identity has been completely trans-

Figure 2: The continuum of ascribed–achieved religion

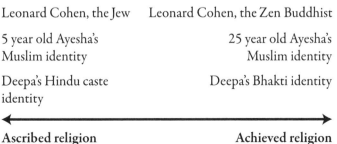

Leonard Cohen, the Jew	Leonard Cohen, the Zen Buddhist
5 year old Ayesha's Muslim identity	25 year old Ayesha's Muslim identity
Deepa's Hindu caste identity	Deepa's Bhakti identity

Ascribed religion **Achieved religion**

formed. In Deepa's case we meet a person who is born into a Hindu caste and this religious identity is ascribed by birth, but she also embraces the religiosity offered by a local *bhakti* saint of the kind described in the chapter about Hinduism. This means that in her daily life Deepa very much has a traditional religious identity that is hard to change, but whenever she visits her saint and engages with her devotional community, she has a religious identity that she has chosen freely, which is achieved and may be changed according to her wishes. I have put these three people in a simple figure for the sake of illustration.

PART 3

THE PRESENT—SEVEN SINS OF
GOVERNMENT INTERVENTION

9

CROWDING OUT

WHEN GOVERNMENT KILLS INITIATIVE

I never donate anything to my local church in Oslo because the Norwegian state funds the established Church of Norway and all other registered religious organizations in the country. But what would I do if the government decided it would no longer provide public funding to religious communities? I certainly would not like to lose my local church. I am not an avid church-goer or a convinced Lutheran, but I like the thought of having a church in my neighborhood to visit on Christmas Day and to carry out my family's rites of passage: christenings, weddings and burials. I also feel that the building itself, a rather large red brick, neo-gothic church built in 1855, infuses a sense of meaning and direction to the local urban geography.

Why subsidize religion?

If the government wants us to eat more apples and smoke fewer cigarettes, it may be sensible to subsidize apples and tax cigarettes. There are good reasons for increasing consumption of apples and decreasing that of cigarettes because we know that this will have an effect on public health. But it is problematic to say that increasing or decreasing the consumption of religion has some positive effect on society as a whole. As I showed in an early chapter, the idea that religion is a public good, that it produces some kind of diffuse social cohesion or moral harmony, probably has no basis in reality, but is rather a deeply ideological argument developed by modern thinkers like the French sociologist Émile Durkheim and the American sociologist Robert N. Bellah building on ideas promoted by the illiberal philosopher Jean-Jacques Rousseau.

One of the best collections of data about the relationship between religion and state worldwide is called the Religion and State (RAS) dataset, which was started by the Israeli scholar Jonathan Fox. This is an excellent place to look for a snapshot of how governments are involved in religious affairs across the world in our time. If we look at RAS data for the year 2008, we find that 81 out of a total of 177 states (45.8 per cent) provide government funding of religious primary or secondary schools or religious educational programs in non-public schools. The most interesting fact is probably the prevalence of such subsidizing in Western democracies. A total of 18 or 27 states (66.7 per cent) categorized as Western democracies give this type of funding. This number is higher than in all other regions of the world. In Asia, 51.7 per cent of states give this kind of funding, while for the Middle East and North Africa and Sub-Saharan Africa, the numbers are 45 per cent and 34.8 per cent respectively.

One important form of subsidy given to religious organizations is for the state to employ clergy and pay their salaries. Among 27 countries that are categorized as Western democracies, 12 states (44 per cent) give official government positions, salaries or other funding for clergy. In the Middle East and North Africa, the number is far higher. Among the 20 countries in this region included in the data, 14 states (70 per cent) fund clergy in the same way. In Asia and Latin America, the percentage of states that fund clergy is 25 per cent and 29 per cent. The great exception is Sub-Saharan Africa, where only 3 out of a total of 45 states fund clergy.

In 2008, 36.7 per cent of the 177 states that are part of the RAS dataset funded the building, maintenance or repairing of religious sites. The percentage varies greatly between regions with only around 15 per cent of Sub-Saharan African states, 65 per cent of states in the Middle East and North Africa and 67.9 per cent of states in the former USSR funding such projects. In Western democracies, 8 out of 27 states (29.6 per cent) do so. We could have included other criteria in our snapshot of present, global government involvement in religious affairs, but this is enough to make the point. States fund religious schools and education, they pay salaries to clergy and they spend money on religious buildings and sites. What are the consequences of this kind of government involvement?

Too much government

One of the central ideas of the market perspective on religion is that competition leads to greater effort among religious leaders to create new products and create new niches to meet unmet demand. In the first chapter, I looked at how Adam Smith and David Hume thought that priests serving in established churches tend to become lazy. One important idea suggested by several economists is that when there are many small suppliers of religious goods, each of them works harder in the face of competition. But this idea is contested and it is not clear that small size means harder work. For example, research on a range of US religious denominations and congregations found that the market share of a congregation has no relationship to the number of hours worked by clergy or other factors of commitment by the suppliers of religious products. Clergy working in small congregations do not necessarily work harder than their colleagues in large congregations.[1]

In 2008, Jonathan Fox and Ephraim Tabory published a study about the consequences of state regulation on religion using data for eighty-one countries gathered from the RAS dataset. The authors looked at how people's religiosity varied according to the degree of state interference in the religious market. Religiosity was operationalized as three things, namely the degree of attendance at religious services, the degree of religious beliefs and the tendency of people to categorize themselves as religious. State regulation was broken down into six broad areas: official support for religion, general restrictions on religion, religious discrimination, religious regulation, legislation regarding religion and, finally, a composite measure of these five variables. Several of these six measures were again broken down into a number of very specific criteria describing how states in today's world interfere with and control religion.[2]

The study concluded that there was a clear relationship between state regulation of religion and the extent to which people attend religious services and the degree to which they consider themselves religious. The more a state intervenes in the religious market and regulates religion, the less people attend services and the less they want to call themselves religious. How can we explain this?

Sometimes the explanation is rather obvious, as when the reputation of a religious establishment is tarnished by its association with the state. Many people are reluctant to practice an official religion when it is associated too closely with a government that lacks political legitimacy. To grasp this point, we can compare four countries, two with large Muslim majorities and two with large Buddhist majorities, but with different relations between state and religion. Both Pakistan and Indonesia have large Muslim majorities, while Thailand and Sri Lanka have large Buddhist majorities. In Pakistan and Thailand, the political legitimacy of the state is intimately connected with established religion. This is partly true also in Indonesia and Sri Lanka, but not to the extreme degree that one finds in Pakistan and Thailand. It seems that people who work for community development in Sri Lanka and Indonesia see religion as important, even necessary, in their work, while people in the same types of organizations in Pakistan and Thailand perceive religion as an obstacle to development because the established faiths—Pakistani Islam and Thai Buddhism—are too closely associated with states that have used religion in manipulative or oppressive ways.[3] The social capital of religious networks can easily be destroyed in an environment where a government appropriates religious concepts, rhetoric or institutions to promote policies or create political legitimacy. But what about democratic states where people generally trust the government? Why does state regulation dampen religious participation in those environments?

Crowding in or out?

To return to my problem at the beginning of the chapter: if my local church suddenly lost its government funding, I would start to donate money. I know roughly how much I would need to pay to keep the institution running if public funding stopped. The math is relatively simple. The price per person to run the Church of Norway—salaries to employees, maintenance of buildings and so on—is the total cost divided by the number of members. It would amount to around 250 euros per person per year. Currently, the funding is collected through taxes, as it has been for a very long time, just like in most countries with established churches.

How should we make sense of the fact that I don't voluntarily pay a single Norwegian krone to my local church because I know funding is taken care of by the state? Perhaps I am just a miserly person, but that would not be a very interesting explanation. I think we can get at least part of the answer if we look at the growing research literature about the effects of public spending on private donations in different sectors and the overlapping literature about the role of governments in the creation of social capital.

Religion has been one of the main sources of social capital in history. This has been pointed out by many, perhaps most famously by the American sociologist Robert Putnam in his widely read book called *Bowling Alone*, where he discusses the erosion of social capital in the United States. Activities like organizing the collection of money for a new church or singing in a choir create social networks that are valuable to individuals and to society. For many people in the Christian world, religion means participation not only in activities that are strictly and narrowly religious. Many Christians take part in Christian associations where they pick up new skills and new knowledge and where they meet people who can open doors in the job market, for instance. Unfortunately, there is little research about the role of religion in the creation of social capital outside the Western world, but some studies indicate that the tendency is very much the same in Muslim societies: Muslims who participate in religious associations, which does not include their strictly religious activity in mosques, are more likely to engage in the broader civil life of their society.[4]

But there is a conflict in the research about the effects that public funding has on voluntary giving. One side believes that state funding and voluntary donations in civil society tend to compete so that when the state funds something, voluntary contributions to the same thing will go down. Voluntary contributions do not have to be money—hours spent repairing a community building, or training a bunch of kids on a football team, are also important types of donations that mean a lot to the general wealth and happiness of most societies. The other side in this conflict believes that state funding does not compete with voluntary contributions. On the contrary, state funding makes private individuals more likely to contribute with their own time and money, so that the effect of public funding on private contributions is positive. One side talks about the state crowding out private initiative, the other talks about public involvement as crowding in private contributions.

Both sides agree that private contributions and engagement in civil society is positive in itself because it generates social capital. Social capital is the value of the communal networks and the participation of people in society. There has been a lot of research about social capital in recent years, and everybody agrees that societies characterized by dense social networks across cultural or socio-economic groups have more trust, less crime and several other good things. It would be hard to disagree with these general ideas. The question is how best to ensure that the institutional environment fosters these kinds of networks and behaviors. What policies are best suited to create a thriving civil society?

An example could be funding the building or maintenance of an art museum. Those who believe that the state tends to crowd out private contributions will argue that public funding should be used sparingly and conservatively. Those who believe that public funding will crowd in private contributions will see state funds as a necessary tool to create an environment for participation and engagement. The goals are the same—to get the museum up and running and to foster engagement in civil society—but the ideas of the role of public policy to realize the goals are different, even opposed.

There are many details in the research literature about the roles of government in civil society and social capital, but if we now move to the sphere of civil society that we call religion, we can narrow our focus down a bit. Some research suggests that when the state funds religious organizations, the private sense of engagement and responsibility tends to suffer—like my tendency to take my local church for granted. For example, one study of twenty-four European countries finds that the amount of private donations and the willingness to work in a religious organization decrease when the organization receives public funding. This entails an erosion of social capital.[5]

Another study, on Methodist congregations in the United States, found that an expansion of government funding for a particular program of social security in the early 1990s crowded out charitable spending by the churches in a substantial way.[6] The problem with much of the research about the links between government funding and social capital is that both the nature of the societies and communities in question and the nature of the public funding are crucial in determining the effects funding has in a particular context. It is difficult to say anything conclusive and general about the crowding out effect, but a lot of the research concludes that public funding of religion can and often does result in a withdrawal of private initiative and an erosion of social capital.

Size matters

We cannot leave this issue quite yet because it is too important. Whether state funding of religious organizations crowds in or crowds out private donations and engagement, and whether it creates or destroys social capital, is clearly relevant to government policies in this sector. We need to know the right answer if we are interested in the right political management of religion. The problem is that this is not an "either/or" question. When a lot of studies yield what seems to be opposite results, we should expect that the answer is more complex. There certainly is some kind of relationship between public subsidies to religious organizations and the level of private donations. We have good reasons to assume that the level of private donations to a religious organization is a function of both government funding and other factors. Private donations rise or fall in some kind of relationship with the amount of public subsidies because private individuals will take these subsidies into account when deciding whether they really need to give away their own money.

Let us try to illustrate this point with an example. Say you belong to a mosque or church that wants to establish a religious school where children can learn about their religion in evening classes. You know that the cost of running the school will be 100,000 euros per year. This will pay rent, salaries, heating and other necessary things. If your funding runs short of this target, you will have to offer fewer classes and accept fewer kids to your school. Let us also assume that you are good at communicating the educational goals and the funding needs of your school, so that the members of your religious community are informed about the most important aspects of the project. Finally, let us assume that a majority of the community really likes your idea.

The year when the school opens, the government gives you no support at all, but the community contributes with 50,000 in private donations. You are running short of your target and the school cannot run at the level you want this year. The next year, the government gives you 10,000 after you have lobbied the local county office. The private donations rise to 60,000 this year, so your total income is 70,000 euros. You are a bit closer to your target of 100,000. The third year, public subsidies rise to 20,000. You have lobbied more. Private donations go up to 70,000 because you have lobbied in your local community as well. In these three first years, then, public subsidies have crowded in private donations. The community has sensed that your school is a good project and the public funding has lent some prestige and given members the feeling that this is serious and long term.

In the fourth year, public subsidies rise to 30,000, but now private money falls to 60,000. You are still struggling to get the 100,000 euros you need. In the fifth year, the government decides to step up subsidies to 40,000, and private donations fall to 50,000. Over the next few years public funding keeps rising, but private donations continue to fall. What is happening? Public funding is now crowding out private donations because members of your religious com-

munity have started seeing the school as a semi-public institution and do not feel that their contributions are crucial to
its survival. As the founder and head of the school, what
should you do? If government funds keep rising, private
donations will continue to fall. This may give you financial
security, but at the same time it will destroy the feelings of
responsibility and engagement that you relied on from the
community to start the school. Public subsidies are transforming the attitudes of the local community.

This little thought experiment gives an idea—although
grossly simplified—of what is actually going on in the relationship between public funding and private donations in
religious organizations in the real world.[7] The question is not
simply whether government money crowds in or out private
money, but rather how much funding and perhaps what
kinds of subsidies. Figure 3 provides an idealized illustration
of the phenomenon of the non-linear relationship between
public subsidies and private funding.

If you happen to be a leader in a local religious community, this kind of dynamic relationship between public and
private money should matter to you. You could continue to
work to increase or simply keep a high-level of public fund-

Figure 3: Private donations and public subsidies

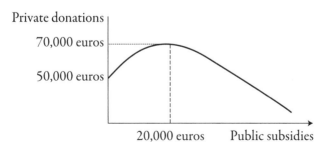

ing, but there are several problems with this strategy. First of all, private donations will decrease when public funds increase, and if public funding covers all the costs of running your operation, private individuals will know and stop donating. This is what happens to me and most other Scandinavians. The church is just another part of the welfare state and we don't care all that much about it apart from the times we need a priest to bury our parents or solemnize our marriages. I know that my local church is completely funded by public money and this is the reason I never give. This is not only a question about money but also about basic human motivation. If I had to donate to my local church and spend some time painting a few walls or organizing meetings for kids, I would probably feel a stronger attachment. This type of involvement is what creates social capital.

What are the political implications of this? First of all, it seems likely that the massive public subsidies given to the national churches of Europe have a negative effect on religious social capital. Private donations are low in many of these societies compared to countries where the running of religious schools and churches is more reliant on private initiative. This in itself could be an argument for being careful about funding religious organizations. As it is entirely possible that a little bit of the right public funding actually crowds in private money and creates civil society engagement, this is not a sufficient argument for cutting all kinds of public support. But as we shall see in the next chapter, there are different problems with government favoritism in the religious market, like rent-seeking and a drift towards monopoly or oligopoly. The different arguments taken together make a strong case for less government involvement and less public funding.

10

RENT-SEEKING

RELIGIONS JOCKEYING FOR PRIVILEGE

In March 2014, *The Economist* published an article with something they called a "crony-capitalism index."[1] Crony-capitalism is a situation where big players in a market can earn more money by influencing politicians and regulators. Most English dictionaries define cronyism as "partiality to long-standing friends"—the word crony is derived from the Greek words for time (*khronos*) and for long-lasting (*khronios*). Crony-capitalism is a major problem in many countries. In *The Economist*'s index, Hong Kong, Russia and Malaysia top the chart, but other rich and developed economies also suffer from cronyism. The importance of cronyism varies between industries. Sectors with much licensing and state involvement are particularly at risk. *The Economist*'s index includes banks, real estate, defense, telecoms services and a number of other sectors where connections with political authorities are important for firms. Cronyism is a problem because it entails rent-seeking and often corruption.

State cronyism and religion

The majority of states in the world display strong partiality to long-standing friends in the religious sector, but for historical reasons we are accustomed to the fact that this particular sector has no place for impartiality. We see state cronyism as the rule of the game in the market for religion. Imagine a cronyism index for the religious markets in different countries across the world—which states would top the list? That would obviously depend on how we choose to define cronyism, but countries where laws, regulations, taxes and subsidies clearly favor one or a few groups or organizations would get the highest scores. Making such a list might take as its point of departure the work that has already been done by scholars to create international criteria for measuring government favoritism of religion, which would probably place certain autocratic and Muslim majority states like Saudi Arabia and Iran at the top of the league.[2]

A fundamental rule of a liberal democracy with a fair economic order is that persons, firms and organizations should expect neutrality and equal treatment when they encounter the state's many faces in the form of law enforcement, regulation or taxation. It is something of a paradox that a great number of states that think of themselves as liberal, including Western democracies, continue to treat religious groups differently.

Why is partiality and cronyism bad for the religious economy? Subsidies and other favors for one or a few selected religious organizations create incentives for dominant religious groups to keep others out of the market and maintain their favored position, and they create incentives for smaller and less favored groups to behave in ways that make them eligible for funding. When the impartiality and neutrality of the state towards religious organizations can be questioned, there will be negative effects. Rent-seeking is a case in point.

Rent-seeking is the work that people or firms do in the political arena in order to secure benefits and privileges for themselves. Rent-protection is the work that goes into keeping privileges that are already in place, but for simplicity we can just use the word rent-seeking for both types of practice. A typical case of rent-seeking is when a large and powerful firm uses its position to make a government or a regulatory authority prevent new entrants to the market. In this way, the firm can secure its own power in the market, and perhaps even achieve a monopoly position. Rent-seeking can also mean engaging in lobbying or offering bribes to officials in order to make authorities behave in ways that are beneficial to the firm. The firm may spend a lot of resources in making its case and thus the resources it can spend to produce its goods must necessarily shrink accordingly. In other words, rent-seeking creates no value. In the economic literature there is a lot of research about the effects of rent-seeking and it is well established that in many countries this kind of activity creates substantial losses to the economy as a whole.

The dangers of rent-seeking are present in the religious market as well. In fact, rent-seeking is so widespread that we have come to see it as part of the normal activity of religious organizations. Think of the public debates and lobbying that religious organizations engage in to expand their own rights and privileges. When religious organizations and individuals spend their resources lobbying, they cannot spend the same resources creating the religious goods consumers of religion want from them. There is a waste of resources and a net loss to society, which is never discussed simply because it is not on most people's radar. The waste that results from rent-seeking is a purely economic argument for keeping a distance between religion and politics.

Just as in other markets, the danger that organizations will engage in rent-seeking is greater when they realize that something can be gained from such activities because government can be influenced by their arguments. It is a symptom of bad policies when religious organizations engage in rent-seeking because it means that policies open the door for this kind of activity or it means that political regulation is sufficiently biased or unclear as to create the impression that rent-seeking will pay off. To illustrate how rent-seeking works in the market for religion I want to present three simple cases from different parts of the world. I choose examples of rent-seeking where the dominant religious establishment has gone to the extreme of forming political parties that have gained influence in politics on a platform almost exclusively devoted to protecting and enhancing the market position of the religious organization or community of religious specialists represented by the party.

Jewish rent-seeking in Israel

My first example comes from Israel. Religiosity in a narrow sense was not important for most of the early Zionists who created the State of Israel, but from the 1980s religious parties moved to the center stage in the country's politics. The National Religious Party (NRP) has been a partner in many government coalitions from its founding in 1956. It was a nationalist religious party with voters both from the Ashkenazi and Sephardic communities, but it lost many of its Sephardic supporters to the Shas party,[3] an ultra-orthodox political party founded in 1984. Sephardic Jews mostly hail from Spain and North Africa whereas Ashkenazi Jews have their geographic and cultural origins in north and central Europe. Ashkenazi Jews have always dominated political and cultural life in Israel. In 2008, the NPR merged with a newly established party, The Jewish Home, which currently has twelve seats in the Knesset and is part of the government coalition with Benjamin Netanyahu as prime minister.

The Shas movement entered the public scene in Israel in the elections to the Knesset (the Israeli parliament) in 1984. Shas is a political party that defends the interests of Sephardic Jews, but it is also a broader and more complex movement that can be analyzed from the point of view of economic and social hierarchies in Israeli society, as well as within the context of ultra-orthodox religiosity and identity.[4] It owes much of its success to its charismatic spiritual head, Rabbi Ovadia Yosef. A third political party, Agudat Yisrael, represents the Ashkenazi ultra-orthodox community. In order to exert influence in politics, Agudat Yisrael has joined forces with another small ultra-orthodox party called Degel HaTorah; together they have formed the United Torah Judaism party, which won seven seats in the Knesset in the 2013 elections.

The importance of religious politics in Israel grew rapidly in the late 1980s and early 1990s, and after the 1996 elections the three religious parties constituted the largest ever religious bloc in the Israeli parliament: Shas won ten seats, NPR won nine and United Torah Judaism four seats. That year, Likud Prime Minister Benjamin Netanyahu formed a new government and included all three religious parties in his administration. They used their new political power to make demands on the Likud party for a stricter interpretation of Jewish law and observance of the Sabbath, a narrower definition of Jewish identity and, most importantly, for substantial increases in government funding for their own institutions, especially religious schools.[5] The religious parties have also been consistent in their support for the expansion of settlements in the West Bank for religious reasons.

Many of the representatives of the religious parties in Israel received a religious education at religious schools (*yeshivas*) and their main political interests are in the area of religious law and education, although some of them have also worked on questions of finance, health, defense and other areas. For instance, Rabbi Yakov Litzman, an experienced politician and religious scholar who heads the United Torah Judaism party in the Knesset, has been deputy minister of health. A fundamental concern of rent-seeking firms is to influence authorities to keep competitors out of the market and this has been an important concern for the religious parties in Israel. In 2007, Yacov Margi, the leader of Shas in the Knesset, proposed a bill that would make all proselytism in Israel illegal and punishable with one year in prison. The bill was put forward on the instruction of Rabbi Ovadia Yosef. This and other Jewish initiatives against proselytism are motivated by fears that Jews will convert to Christianity or Islam and that this will undermine the survival of Judaism in the long run.

In the 2013 election campaign, the ultra-orthodox parties in Israel focused on identity politics. They expressed concerns over the relaxation of religious requirements for conversion to Judaism and over the immigration of secular Russian Jews. More relevant to my discussion of rent-seeking, however, is the fact that both Shas and the United Torah Judaism party were very concerned, as they have been in previous election campaigns, with the opposition from sections of Israeli society to the privileges enjoyed by the ultra-orthodox communities. They want to keep their exemption from military service and retain government funding for religious schools.

Buddhist rent-seeking in Sri Lanka

Some of the most glaring examples of religious rent-seeking today can be observed in the Buddhist world. My second example consequently comes from Sri Lanka. Sri Lanka is an island state at the southern tip of the Indian subcontinent. It has a Buddhist majority population of just over 70 per cent, while 12.6 per cent are Hindu, 9.7 per cent are Muslim and 6.1 per cent are Catholic.[6] As we saw in the chapter about the Buddhist world, Sri Lankan society has been characterized by a close relationship between government and the order of Buddhist monks for many centuries. The Buddhist order has enjoyed a number of privileges in Sri Lankan society and the monks have played important roles as ritual specialists, as teachers and as a field in which laypeople can sow their good deeds and harvest religious merit according to the law of karma.

Ever since Sri Lanka gained its independence from Britain in 1948, the relationship between religion and politics has been the subject of intense debate. In particular, after the beginning of the civil war in 1983, the position of Buddhist monks in political life changed with a number of leading monks taking political initiatives that would traditionally have been outside the scope of the life of religious specialists. In 2004, a new political party entered the Sri Lankan political stage. It is called the Jathika Hela Urumaya (JHU), which roughly means National Heritage Party. In the April elections to the Sri Lankan parliament that year, the JHU put forward more than 260 monks as candidates for the 225 seats, and their candidates won nine seats. Having monks in parliament was a novelty in the Buddhist world.

The JHU ran on a political platform that firmly rejected talk of devolving power to Tamil separatists in the north of the island as a solution to the war and insisted on preserving the political integrity and unity of the island. They also demanded *dharmarajya*, a polity (*rajya*) based on *dharma*. *Dharma* can mean many different things, but in this context it meant religious and moral order. What the monk-politicians in the JHU wanted was a government that shaped policies according to specifically Buddhist conceptions of moral order and they were extremely concerned about what they perceived as a steady decline of Buddhist culture in Sri Lanka that could be traced back to the foreign influence of colonial times as well as to new challenges from globalization. They wanted to re-introduce "proper" Buddhism into all sections of society, perhaps most importantly in the field of education. They wanted the curricula of schools to be adjusted so as to teach children and adolescents Sinhalese Buddhist culture and values concerning religion, history and national identity, and issues like the proper relations between monks and laypeople and between different family members.

Most of the JHU's political concerns were about the status of Buddhism in Sri Lankan society and this was perhaps most clear in their initiatives to make "unethical conversions" illegal in the country. Among sections of the Buddhist monkhood and Sinhalese society more generally there was deep concern about the activities of Christian evangelical missionaries working in the island. These concerns were formulated by the superstar monk Venerable Soma who died in December 2003. Soma was a very popular public monk with his own shows on national TV and a large following among Sinhalese Buddhists. One of his main concerns was to stop the conversion of Buddhists to Christianity. According to Soma and the monks in the JHU, as well as activists in other Buddhist organizations, foreign evangelical groups and individuals were settling in Sri Lanka and registering as NGOs only to tempt poor Buddhists to convert to Christianity by offering material benefits.[7] The debate about a bill making such "unethical conversions" illegal has raged in Sri Lanka for some time now.

The politics of the JHU is a good example of rent-seeking in a modern Buddhist majority society because their political program is generally limited to securing the benefits and the cultural and social status that Buddhism has enjoyed for a long time and to raising the barriers to entry of competing religions.

Muslim rent-seeking in Pakistan

Pakistan was born in 1947 as the British pulled out of India and divided the enormous colony into two states. Muslim nationalist leaders had successfully lobbied for a separate homeland for the Muslims of South Asia for some time. The people who made the creation of Pakistan possible were intellectual Muslim nationalists, like Muhammed Ali Jinnah and Muhammed Iqbal. They were convinced that the Muslims of South Asia constituted a nation in need of their own state, but they did not plan to create an Islamic state of the kind that was later developed during the dictatorship of General Zia ul-Haq, who seized power in a coup in 1977 and ruled until 1988.

What was the role of Islam and the religious elite in the early politics of Pakistan? Maulana Maududi (1903–79) was the most formidable revivalist thinker in South Asia in the twentieth century and he exerted great influence on politics throughout the Islamic world. He was born in Aurangabad in India to a prominent Muslim family and became a prolific journalist and writer. Maududi worked all his life to realize what he believed was a good society based on Islamic ideals and vision of politics. Maududi received a religious education from the most respected madrasa in Muslim India located at Deoband, but he was ambivalent about his own standing as a religious scholar. He was well aware that Muslim scholars, the class of people known as the ulama, had kept out of politics through most of Islamic history and left the business of governing society to sultans and caliphs.

The role of the religious elite had been to give legitimacy to political rulers and to offer a range of religious, educational and legal services to society, not unlike the roles of religious elites in Christian or Jewish societies. To Maududi, the traditional separation of religion and politics was a bad idea and a deviation from the very earliest visions of the Islamic system formulated by the Prophet Muhammad and the first caliphs who followed him as head of the community. He wanted to return to what he saw as the original Islamic vision according to which religion and politics were one. For this reason, he was often very critical of the passive role of the religious elites in modern South Asia and in most of Islamic history.

The answer was to engage wholeheartedly in modern party politics. In August 1941, Maulana Maududi gathered seventy leading Muslims in the city of Lahore, in today's Pakistan, and founded a new political party called Jamaat-e-Islami or Jamaat for short. In the mind of Maududi and his followers, the Jamaat was both a political party and a holy community of devout and learned Muslims. It was built on the idea that to be a proper Muslim one had to be highly educated and have the intellectual ability to understand Islamic law and the Quran. This was a highly elitist vision about the role of religious scholars in politics, which was radically different from Muslim nationalist parties with more or less secular ideas about the proper relationship between religion and politics, like the Muslim League of Jinnah.

From its foundation, the Jamaat played an important role in Pakistani politics. As the leader, or amir, of the party, Maududi saw himself as the head of a new kind of Muslim community, the *Ummah*, that was both religious and political at the same time. Several of Maududi's closest aides were also educated members of the *ulama*. This was the case for Muhammad Manzoor Nomani, for example, a co-founder of the Jamaat who competed with Maududi for the position as leader. In fact, if we check the names of the first group of people who came together in 1941 to found the Jamaat, a great many of them have titles like Maulana or Maulvi, meaning they have formal religious education and belong to the ulama.[8] The point is that the new type of political party the Jamaat represented attracted the participation of a large number of religious scholars. In line with their elitist visions of Islamic political and religious leadership, they spent much of their working lives lobbying the government for privileges for their segment of society and their own faith instead of engaging in the traditional tasks of religious scholars in Muslim societies.

What are the consequences? It seems to me that this kind of rent-seeking behavior by the Muslim elites in Pakistan has helped lay the foundations for an alliance between government and religion that has become detrimental to the freedom of religious minorities and provided legitimacy for religious persecution. The Jamaat is certainly not the only organization to blame for this development—in fact, they were critical of the undemocratic policies of General Zia despite his efforts to Islamize Pakistan—but there is a widespread feeling among religious elites of dominant Sunni Islam that they have legitimate claims on the government. This has created a culture of majoritarian entitlement to cultural and religious hegemony, which we find also in the religious parties in Israel and Sri Lanka discussed in this chapter.

The trouble with religious political parties

I have briefly presented cases of religious rent-seeking: ultra-orthodox parties in Israel, a nationalist monk-party in Sri Lanka and an Islamic party in Pakistan. All these parties are organized by religious specialists—rabbis, monks, ulama—who work to achieve explicit goals: to maintain the privileged position of their religion in laws and regulations, to keep and expand subsidies and other privileges given to them by the state and to stop possible competitors from entering the religious markets they dominate.

The most important privileges they seek are often about the status of religion in law and especially in national constitutions. It is not a coincidence that all the religious parties I have looked at in this chapter have spent a lot of energy lobbying their respective governments for more favorable treatment of the dominant religion and its organization in the constitutions of these states. Other important privileges they lobby for include subsidies for religious institutions, especially educational institutions, but they are also concerned with the way religion and culture is presented in public discourse and in school curricula. It is revealing that all these parties work to create barriers for the entry of competitors by making it illegal to carry out missionary work by religious groups other than themselves.

Because these religious political parties are fundamentally rent-seeking firms, religious politics in these cases shares several characteristics despite the fact that the cultural and political contexts are very different. In the cases presented here, agitation on the part of religious parties has been a major illiberal force in the countries in question. Israeli, Sri Lankan and Pakistani politics have been pushed in the direction of religious nationalism and chauvinism. The elites representing a religious majority feel strongly that their own religious tradition is entitled to special treatment. Their goal seems to be the religious and cultural hegemony of a dominant tradition. Tolerance for other religions or for other interpretations of the dominant religion has declined accordingly.

The effective way to change this is to look at these political parties and the religious organizations they represent in the same way as we look at firms in other markets and apply policies designed to counter rent-seeking activities and their negative consequences. A radical but effective road to take would be for the parliaments of these states to change the relationship between religious organizations and the state. If the scope for subsidies and other privileges was removed, or at least narrowed considerably, and if the Jewish, Buddhist and Muslim majorities were told unambiguously that their respective religious groups and their organizations would no longer enjoy a favored relationship with the state, then the incentives for rent-seeking would decrease.

There is a reason why I picked relatively recent examples to illustrate religious rent-seeking. We can safely assume that representatives of powerful religious groups have been engaged in lobbying, agitation and bribes directed at political leaders throughout history. Their goals have been to achieve or maintain legislation and regulations that privilege themselves in the religious market, to get subsidies or other kinds of material support and to strengthen the barriers to the market in order to prevent competitors from entering. With the global political changes that took place after the Second World War, the political game changed in many parts of the world and this was certainly the case in the countries I looked at here. From the 1940s and 50s, newly founded states worked to implement some form of parliamentary democracy. Some were successful and some were not. The new political game created new rules. The ultraorthodox parties in Israel, the monk-party in Sri Lanka and the Islamist party in Pakistan illustrate how religious groups adjust their rent-seeking activities to fit modern political systems. Religious leaders who often belong to conservative traditions that are fundamentally skeptical when it comes to modern electoral politics throw themselves into the political game for purely pragmatic reasons. They hold their noses and become politicians.

11

MONOPOLY

NORDIC STATE CHURCHES
AND COMMUNIST REPRESSION

There is no doubt in my mind about what is the most pleasant way to observe a religious state monopoly in the world today: go to Denmark, travel around the flat, green countryside and visit some of the country's ancient white churches. It is not so much that the Danes are crazy about their state church; they are just not able to envisage civilized life without it. The last chapter was about the problems related to rent-seeking. Religious organizations and leaders spend resources pursuing privileges, and governments spend resources in designing and enforcing regulation. These resources are lost to society. When rent-seeking is successful, it leads to market structures with one or very few powerful firms. This sometimes results in a monopoly. But what exactly do we mean by monopoly in the religious markets of our own times? Much of the economic research about contemporary religion uses the term without discussing precisely what it means.

What is a religious monopoly or oligopoly?

Much of the debate about the merits of the market approach to religion has revolved around the concept of diversity and there is good reason to assume that a high degree of diversity leads to greater consumption of religion. Diversity gives the consumer more choice. In the economic and legal literature on how to enhance competition and avoid monopolization of markets, a key factor in determining the market power of a supplier of a product is the availability of alternative products. If the consumer wants the product offered by the monopolist and there is no alternative on the market, the market power is higher than in a situation where the consumer can substitute her product with a slightly different and less expensive product. We can talk about this as the price elasticity of demand, which is an expression of how easily a consumer is able to switch to a substitute product. The higher the elasticity (i.e. the easier it is for a consumer to choose an alternative), the smaller the monopoly power of the dominant firm. One way for a dominant religious organization to strengthen its power in a market, then, is to make it more difficult for people to switch allegiance, in other words to lower the elasticity of demand.

Elasticity of demand should be a crucial concept in our analysis of religious markets and the concept should ideally include all kinds of barriers against switching religious affiliations. These barriers can be of several types. There can be legal constraints on converting, but these often interact with cultural and social forces that are critical of conversion and wish to limit freedom of religion. This is the case in many Islamic states and there are important discussions going on in many Muslim communities about the unreasonableness of denying people the right to change religions and the madness of punishing apostasy. There have been high-profile cases of death-sentences for apostasy in Pakistan and Afghanistan over the past few years. The increasing religious intolerance that can be observed in sections of Pakistani society is more a product of the abuse of Islam as a political tool that started in the 1970s, especially under General Zia, than it is an expression of timeless Islamic principles, but this is a discussion that would lead us too far afield.

The fact that some governments still see traditional punishment for apostasy as applicable is a challenge to religious freedom and human rights. Fortunately, things can be changed, as proved for instance by the Islamic Council of Norway, an umbrella association uniting most of the Muslim organizations in the country. They have formally declared that they support the basic human right to leave Islam. Cultural, legal and political currents against conversion are also strong in countries like Israel, India, Sri Lanka and Greece, to name just a handful representing different world religions.

If we return to our historical examples, we observed that very effective barriers to entry can be raised under a number of different political conditions and do not rely in any way on the exceptional coercive power of the modern state. The medieval Catholic Church created barriers to entry by branding competition as heresy and making it punishable. The Church had a formidable asset in its ecclesiastical laws and in the fact that Church officials doubled as secular rulers with their own armies. In the Buddhist world, barriers to entry varied enormously between different societies. We saw that in Tibet, after Mahayana Buddhism became a state religion, other Buddhist denominations and other religions could effectively be kept out with the use of military force. In Theravada Buddhist societies in Thailand, Burma and Sri Lanka, the official form of Buddhism was extremely closely associated with royal power. All the symbols of political power were also Buddhist symbols. However, we saw that the major barrier to entry was probably the institution of exchange in which common people could secure a favorable rebirth only by interacting in an institutionalized manner with representatives of official Buddhism. The institutionalized exchange of goods from the laity against "spiritual" or "religious" goods from the monks and nuns rests on the worldview of karma.

A free religious market requires three things. First, there must be a certain degree of diversity. Secondly, there must be low barriers to entry. Thirdly, there must be a certain degree of elasticity of demand. Therefore, we can define a religious monopoly as a market structure of organizations supplying religious goods in which (1) one supplier has a very large market share, (2) there are high legal and/or cultural barriers to entry, and (3) there is low elasticity of demand. This definition shows that the question of monopoly versus free markets is seldom either/or. There is a sliding scale going from a completely free market to a pure monopoly and if we want to place a particular geographical or historical market on this scale, we need to consider the details of each case on its own merits.

The most widespread state of affairs in the religious markets across the world today is probably not monopoly, but oligopoly, which is where two, or a very limited number of firms, share the market with high barriers to entry and low elasticity of demand. The only part of the definition that would change from monopoly is the word "one" in the first criteria above. It would be possible to use my definition of monopoly to list the states of the world on a sliding scale by making the three criteria operational. One would need to count the number of suppliers and measure their market share and one would need to measure the barriers to entry. This could best be done by using databases that contain data about how governments regulate religion and especially about the criteria for registering a new religious organization. Measuring elasticity of demand would probably be slightly more difficult because it contains both formal hindrances and far more subtle cultural barriers against switching religious affiliations.

Black and gray markets

In the Communist states governments worked hard to suppress or abolish religion. Karl Marx, the ideological father of Communism, was convinced that what really matters to human civilization is how we produce our own means of existence and how the economy is organized. Marx was a materialist and objected strongly to other thinkers who said that religion or other ideas played an independent role in history and society. According to Marx, the history of mankind must be understood according to how ownership of capital is distributed in society. In our stage of history, capitalists own factories and hire workers to labor long hours in order to enrich the owners. In Marxism, religion is part of an all-embracing ideology that justifies an existing organization of ownership where the rich owners of land or factories exploit their laborers and extract value from their work. At the same time, it is also an expression of suffering and a protest against suffering by the downtrodden, Marx wrote. Religion is the sigh of the oppressed. It is the task of critical thinking and writing to show that religion is illusory happiness and real happiness requires that we give up such illusions.

In the Marxist vision, therefore, it is important to get rid of religion. It is a veil that hides real injustice and hampers historical progress towards the Communist utopia. The tactics and policies that Communist governments used to achieve this varied widely according to place and time, from killing religious elites and bulldozing religious buildings under Stalin and Mao to the softer repression in East Germany (GDR), or under later Soviet and Chinese governments. Repression of religion under Communism was often accompanied by state-sanction of one or a selected range of official religions that were closely watched and regulated by the authorities. Many Communist officials took a realistic approach in the sense that they understood people's need for religion. Often this meant that abolishing religious life was pondered as a long-term rather than a short-term goal. Repression of religion was also accompanied by state-supported atheist ideologies that sometimes became substitutes for religion in the sense that they appealed to some of the same cognitive and emotional needs that religion normally satisfies. The pseudo-religious worship of Mao or Lenin is a case in point.

In a book about religion in Communist China, the sociologist Fenggang Yang has developed a model that contains three different markets for religion: red, black and gray.[1] The red market is the handful of religious organizations that are legal, the black market contains the illegal forms of religion, while the gray are all the ambiguous practices that fall between the legal and illegal. In Communist China, the repression of religion went through several stages. The attack on religious institutions and people was at its most harsh between 1966 and 1979 when religion was banned, religious venues closed and religious texts and artifacts destroyed. After 1979, Chinese policies have tolerated some officially recognized religious groups: Buddhism, Daoism, Islam, Protestantism and Catholicism. The government keeps tight control over the recognized and patriotic organizations representing these five religious traditions. Accepted religious activities receive government protection, while the authorities work to stamp out illegal activities.

The legal religious outlets constitute a regulated oligopolistic market, the red market, and participation in this market has increased rapidly over recent decades. But participation in the other two markets is on the rise, too. The black market is the collection of illegal religious organizations and their activities, while the gray market consists of religious and spiritual groups and practices with ambiguous legal status. In the gray market, one typically finds spiritual practices that are manifested—one could perhaps say that they are disguised as—science or medicine and a range of illegal types of spiritualities and folk religious practices carried out in secret by legal religious organizations. The lively religious and spiritual life that takes place in the black and gray markets under Communist repression indicates not only that it is hard to get rid of religion but also that religious demand will always exist and will always create new markets and new niches if the normal outlets are blocked by the state.

The interesting question is whether the volume and reach of the black and gray markets are a function of the level of repression and regulation in the red market. If the forms of religious life in the legal market are restricted, people will find religious products that match their demand in the black and gray markets. As Fenggang Yang points out, when the red market is limited and the suppression of the black market is severe, the gray market will necessarily grow. It seems to me that this is a good way to analyze what happens when governments create monopolies and oligopolies in general, not only in Communist states. One could, for instance, talk about green, black and gray markets in some Muslim majority states where religious groups other than official Islam are repressed. The idea of a legal, an illegal and an ambiguous market could also be applied to historical cases, like the monopolistic Protestant churches of Scandinavia.

The Scandinavian state churches

"It is a fact of history that people [folk] and church have grown together in Denmark, as in the other Scandinavian countries," wrote Henrik Christiansen, a former bishop of the Danish city of Aalborg in an essay about church-belonging in Scandinavian societies.[2] The bishop was right: there is a Siamese twin-like quality to the relationship between people and church in Scandinavia. The degree to which people belong to the official Lutheran churches of Denmark, Sweden and Norway is remarkable.

Things have slowly started to change, though. In 2000, Sweden cut its old ties between state and church. But the Swedish Church is still called the folk church, which means the people's church. In 2012, a significant change was made to the Constitution of Norway that ended the special status of the Lutheran church as the official church of the state. Still, the Norwegian constitution calls the Lutheran church the country's folk church, the state pays the bill for most of the church's expenses and the king has a constitutional relationship to the church. The Swedish folk church still has a prominent position in society and in Swedish national identity and it is my experience from lecturing about these matters a number of times in Denmark that most Danes do not understand what you mean if you ask about their views on the state church. To the Danes, the Church of Denmark is a natural branch of the state, and only a staunch minority with self-consciously liberal or libertarian outlooks see the state church as a threat to religious equality and freedom.[3]

The road to religious monopoly in Scandinavia is complex, but the natural starting point for a brief historical background is the Reformation. From 1397, the three countries had been part of a political union, the Kalmar Union, which was destroyed when Swedish King Gustav Vasa initiated a Swedish war of liberation and was elected king of Sweden on 6 June 1523. This date is the national day of Sweden. In Denmark, the 1520s and 30s were a period of internal strife, while in Norway there were forces that were seeking to gain Norwegian independence from Denmark.

Danish King Fredrik I was a Catholic, but his son Christian became a zealous Lutheran. Christian became a Lutheran after meeting Martin Luther in April 1521, when Luther publicly defended his critical writings about the Catholic Church in the German city of Worms. Luther had been called to Worms by Emperor Carl V and the public hearing was carried out by the Catholic theologian Johann von Eck. Urged by Eck to recant, Luther famously refused to revoke the heresies contained in his many books, but he was able to escape from the town before the papal representative had formulated the condemnation of Luther, which was published in the imperial Edict of Worms on 25 May 1521. The edict outlawed even the possession of Luther's works and called for the immediate arrest of the obstinate reformer.

In the spring of that year, Luther was a rock star in the making. The young Count Christian simply loved Martin Luther, like a lot of northern Europeans were starting to do around this time. As count of Haderslev county, Christian invited theologians from Luther's circle in Wittenberg to come and start a local reformation of the church from 1525 onwards. When his father, the king, died in 1533, he continued his policy of Lutheranism and in October 1536 he published a law firing all the Catholic bishops and seizing for the crown all the castles, mansions, forests and fields belonging to the church. In place of the old bishops, he hired new men to run the church and gave them the title of superintendents, making it clear that they were servants of the king. In the same year, 1536, the Norwegian parliament (Riksråd), which had worked so hard to achieve independence, was dissolved by the Danish king, and Norway became a Danish colony once more.

The dramatic political upheavals in Scandinavia during the first decades of the 1500s resulted in two states, Sweden and Denmark–Norway, with Lutheran churches closely associated with the person of the king. The church had lost all independence. Church and state were now two sides of the same coin. Power was increasingly being centralized, which would culminate in what is known as the absolute monarchy of the late 1600s, and the kings used the church in their effort to discipline society. The monarchs felt responsible for the moral and spiritual welfare of the people. It became essential to the fervently religious Danish–Norwegian king to enforce orthodoxy, correct belief and to combat moral corruption, illegal sex, blasphemy and swearing. The Scandinavian churches became a doctrinal, moral and spiritual police force.[4]

The Scandinavian societies had quite similar experiences with religious monopolies in the three centuries following the Reformation, but after the Napoleonic Wars things started to change. In 1814, Denmark had to give Norway to Sweden as compensation for choosing the wrong side in the war. In the same period, new political and ideological currents started to make an impression. From the revolutionary period came the novel idea that human beings were born with rights. Freedom of religion was one of them. Monopolistic state churches were now seen as oppressive and there were movements in all of Scandinavia to allow religious minorities—which only meant Christian sects, like Quakers— to practice their religion freely.

As a result, in the middle of the nineteenth century, the formal religious monopolies of the three societies constituting Scandinavia came to an end. Between 1830 and 1850, all three countries were forced to scrap old laws that banned religious gatherings outside official church sermons and required a minimum church attendance. But even though the official state-sanctioned monopoly was abandoned, the real religious monopoly of the state churches continued well into the twentieth century. Up to 1951, one could not leave the Church of Sweden without simultaneously registering with another religious organization; a range of other incremental legal changes show how the road towards real freedom of religion was a piecemeal affair. There were also some differences between Sweden, Denmark and Norway, and when we enter the modern period the differences become more pronounced. Sweden began to have a serious debate about dis-establishing the state church in the nineteenth century, whereas Denmark did not question the marriage of church and state to the same extent. Norway is somewhere in-between.

Social democracy and the folk

In the political debates about the state church in all three Scandinavian countries, the pivotal rhetorical concept has been the folk church. At the end of the nineteenth and beginning of the twentieth century there were initiatives from within the churches to loosen their ties to the state. Several reformist priests used the concept of a free folk church as the opposite of a stale and illiberal state church. However, after the Second World War the rhetorical contents of the concept of folk church changed, and all the social democratic political parties have decided on policies where they see a tightly controlled state church as the only guarantee that the church can retain its quality as a religious organization embracing the folk, the people, in its totality. The concept of folk church has been appropriated by the social democratic defenders of government control.[5]

The social democratic governments that have ruled Sweden, Denmark and Norway since the Second World War have mostly seen the national churches as instruments of the government to move society in the direction of an inclusive and egalitarian welfare state. They have also been very eager to keep government control over the churches to stop potential conservative forces inside the churches from gaining power. In debates about the future of the state church in Sweden and Norway during the twentieth century, the Swedish Social Democratic Labor Party (SAP) and the Norwegian Labor Party (AP) argued that national churches with too much independence from the state could represent a challenge to liberal theology and to the ideologies of gender equality and church democracy that have been so important in these countries. There was a deep tension in the social democratic ideology of Scandinavia, from its beginnings in the late nineteenth century, between the Marxist idea that the church represented capitalist interests and should be destroyed and a more pragmatic view that the church could serve as a useful instrument in the implementation of social democratic policies. Both the Swedish SAP and the Norwegian AP had several internal battles to determine which ideological direction should influence their church policies, but revolutionaries and hardliners had mostly been sidelined or converted to pragmatics by the 1940s.[6]

Therefore, the social democracies of Scandinavia continued to view the church as a branch of the state to be used by the king, or in our day by a ministry of church affairs, for the control of society. There was certainly more freedom, and old doctrines were questioned from inside the churches in order to keep theology in tune with wider culture, but the ideology that sees people and church as one has grown together over the centuries, and the desire to use the church as a political instrument has continued right down to the present. "Church affairs are much too important to be left to theologians," said Gudmund Hernes, the former minister for church affairs for the Norwegian AP.[7]

Scandinavian history is highly instructive for an economic analysis of religion. We have good reason to believe that the strict and oppressive religious monopolies that the Scandinavian societies experienced from the sixteenth to the nineteenth centuries was one important cause for the steep decline in active participation in official religion during the twentieth century. In all three Scandinavian countries, participation in religious services is now incredibly low and belief in key Christian doctrines, like a personal God or heaven and hell, has been dwindling for some time. Scandinavia has come to be seen as a laboratory for social scientists interested in the long-term effects of religious monopoly on religious participation and beliefs.

Several of the scholars who formulated the basics of the economic approach to religion in the 1980s and 90s all saw

Scandinavia as a part of the world where they could test their ideas about the effects of freedom and monopoly on religious life. They believed that the dwindling church attendance and the marginal role of traditional Christian belief that can be observed in Scandinavia are caused by a lack of competition on the supply-side of the religious equation. A market structure characterized by an absence of religious diversity and the presence of state-funded behemoths of Lutheran folk churches does not create incentives for local churches and staff to develop religious goods and services that might satisfy the latent demand in Scandinavian populations.

Scandinavia is really a gift to scholars who want to test theories about religious demand and supply because these three states have so much data that can be used to check assumptions about the economics of religion. Swedish scholars have used the massive amounts of information collected by the Church of Sweden to show correlations that support the basic theories of the economic approach. If we order all the municipalities of Sweden according to whether they offer few or many religious services, and whether services are mostly traditional Sunday morning services or a more diverse range of services, we see that participation is substantially higher where services are "many and varied" than where services are "few and traditional." Moreover, the local communities in which the Church of Sweden offer many and varied services are more likely to be the communities where there is also a strong presence of free churches.[8] Free churches are small Christian faith groups outside, and often in some tension with, the dominant Church of Sweden, and it seems very reasonable to assume that the presence of such competitors is an incentive for the priests of the Church of Sweden to create both more and more varied services. The data used in this particular research are from 1991 and a lot has happened in the religious sphere in Sweden since then, but that does not undermine the insight that both the amount and diversity of types of religious goods seems to have had a positive effect on religious participation on the local level in Sweden.

In his rearguard action against the advance of the economic approach to religion, sociologist Steve Bruce has claimed that Scandinavia does not fit the economic paradigm at all. He says that the religious monopolies of the Scandinavian state churches were abandoned long ago and if there was anything to the economic theory, which claims that more diversity and competition leads to more consumption of religion, we should have been able to observe increasing participation and belief. It seems to me that key elements in Bruce's critique are misguided, however. He disregards the fact that increasing freedom of religion has not produced religious diversity in Scandinavia. Few people believed that greater religious freedom and the end of the church's monopoly would lead to more consumption if the diversity and quality of the religious products on offer did not increase. Moreover, Bruce dismisses detailed studies of local religious markets, like the one carried out by Swedish scholars discussed above, by saying that these religious markets, where diversity and competition seem to matter in a real way, are not interesting because they exist within a larger picture of secularization. He is saying, then, that he cannot deny that there are religious markets, but this is irrelevant because his own paradigm of general secularization exists on a higher level and encompasses the market dynamics that other scholars have pointed to. This sounds implausible to me.

What is the problem with mega-churches?

In an earlier chapter I argued that defining a religious market is not necessarily more difficult than defining other types of markets, like markets for beer or soft-drinks. A main criticism of the economic analysis of religion builds on the incorrect assumption that defining "normal" markets is easy while delimiting markets for religious services is difficult or impossible. Does beer compete with wine and cider? It may or it may not depending on a range of circumstances. Do the religious goods offered by a Catholic church compete with those offered by a mosque or a synagogue in the same town? Probably not. Most Catholics do not think of Islam or Judaism as very good potential substitutes for their current religion. In most cases, the relevant competition between religious goods in the real world is probably not between those offered by two completely different religious traditions. Muslims or Christians will not see the religious beliefs and rituals of Hinduism as a natural substitute for the beliefs and rituals they are used to. Instead, the relevant market should often be delimited by looking closely at those religious goods that consumers in fact see as substitutes and where there is competition.

The growth of mega-churches in the United States and other parts of the world offers a good illustration of the importance of paying attention to local circumstances when considering religious markets. Mega-churches can be defined as churches with congregations numbering more than 2,000 active members. In the United States, the number of mega-churches has grown rapidly over the past couple of decades. They belong almost exclusively to the evangelical branch of Protestant Christianity. There have been two opposite assumptions among scholars about the effects these big churches have on other Christian churches. One group believes that the big churches will put the little churches out of business because they can offer similar products in a more cost-efficient way, while the opposite view is that the mega-churches will encourage other churches to improve their services in order to compete and survive.

The debate about mega-churches is a bit like the debate over Walmart in the United States. When a huge Walmart store opens its doors in a US town, the smaller shops face fierce competition because Walmart has perfected the art of cutting costs and doing things efficiently. This has caused both politicians and scholars to warn of the death of the mom and pop shop. If we apply the same kind of reasoning to the religious markets in the United States, we should perhaps fear that the rise of the mega-churches will cause the death of most other Christian churches and lead to a situation where American Christianity becomes ever more streamlined, efficient and one-dimensional. From this perspective, a free market creates an opportunity for too much market power and the death of diversity. Perhaps somebody should call for anti-trust action in the sphere of religion.

But if we look closely at the effects of mega-churches it seems that the situation is far more complex and less gloomy. Mega-churches do in fact bring intense competition, but only for churches that operate with very similar products, which means other evangelical churches. Smaller evangelical churches in the vicinity of mega-churches are in fact likely to go out of business because their huge neighbor delivers a product that is similar in a more efficient way. Remember the idea of elasticity of demand. But the effect on non-evangelical Christian churches is the opposite. If you look at mainline Protestant churches, or Catholic churches, or even fundamentalist churches, they experience a positive effect from the presence of mega-churches. In areas where these types of congregations generally lose members, the losses are considerably less severe when a mega-church is present, and in areas where these non-evangelical congregations experience growth, their gains are greater.

The reasonable interpretation would be that local religious markets in the United States contain a number of niches, and real and relative growth and decline in market shares is determined by factors like the way in which producers of slightly different products market their goods and the way in which consumers perceive competing religious goods to be substitutes. Big and small evangelical churches compete in the same market niche and vie for the participation and the money of the same people. Other Christian churches offer a different product in a different niche and do not lose out to evangelical mega-churches. Instead, mainstream Protestants, Catholics and fundamentalists get stimulation from this type of competition. Often they realize that they simply have to specialize, work hard and offer something that the giant evangelical church cannot offer. Even the staunchest opponents of the economic perspective on religion would have to admit that data like these show that we can get important insights from looking at the supply and demand of religion as a market.[9]

12

DISCRIMINATION

WOMEN, GAY PEOPLE AND GOD

If you ever want to start your own religious congregation, here is my advice. Go for a theology that says God is a woman. Create a code of social ethics that emphasizes the rights of women to be public religious leaders, priests, pastors, imams or rabbis, and throw in their right to work in the types of jobs they want, and the obligation of men to be kind and supportive and share household chores. Women are generally more religiously inclined than men. In Catholic, Protestant, Orthodox, Muslim, Buddhist, Hindu and Confucian countries women are generally significantly more likely to count themselves as religious, to believe in God, to pray or meditate and to do other things that we can call religious.[1] Still, the majority of religious organizations worldwide have theologies and codes of ethics that place men above women and demand female submission in the family. Some want women to cover themselves and keep their opinions to themselves, and tell them to take care of the house while the men do the important stuff in public life.

FAITHONOMICS

Market failure, discrimination and freedom of religion

The fact that men occupy almost all positions of power and prestige in religious organizations, and the reality that many women are often denied the religious roles they desire, can be seen as a gigantic market failure. In the language of economics, market failure is a situation where a market fails to allocate goods, services or resources in an efficient way. There can be many reasons for market failure and there can be a wide range of different political answers to them. Sometimes free markets generate market failures and there is an argument for government intervention. A standard example is when a factory pollutes the environment. The pollution is a cost to the rest of society, but without the right regulation the factory will not need to bear the burden for its own pollution. In other cases, a monopoly situation or other types of imperfect market structure lead to market failure and there is an argument for government action to generate more competition. Market failures may call for more or less government intervention depending on the causes.

In practical terms, the world of religion encompasses a huge number of small and large labor markets. People may be hired—or at least compensated in some way—to be Christian clergy, Muslim ulama, Jewish rabbis, Sikh granthis, Hindu pandits or Buddhist monks and they get their salaries, or other types of compensation, from their organization, or sometimes directly from consumers who use their services. It would require a large global survey to prove this, but it is reasonable to say that many, perhaps most, of these small and large religious labor markets are characterized by a market failure resulting from gender discrimination. In particular, the higher positions of religious leadership almost always seem to be reserved for men, either officially or through old practices and precedents.

In the United States, the number of women clergy in the main Christian denominations remains remarkably low. Less than 5 per cent of all head clergy in the Christian churches covered by the large National Congregations Study are women. Women do occupy different types of leadership in US Christian congregations, but these positions are generally of an administrative kind, and the further up the ladder one gets, the greater the male domination.[2] This situation seems to be constant in the sense that the percentage of women clergy in the United States is not increasing, or is doing so very slowly, while women in fact make up the majority of people using the churches. This is something of a paradox. How can it be that women in (presumably) the most free and unregulated market for religion in the world cannot get into positions of power, despite the fact that American women have a considerably higher demand for religious goods than men? Why is male domination such a pervasive feature of American religion if we assume that a really free market would be able to correct itself?

One reply to this could be that the market is in some sort of balance because women do in fact get the religious goods they want. But this is questionable because it is very easy to think of possible religious institutions that would offer theologies and values that would be more attractive to at least some women than those that are often supplied by most American congregations. In particular, the idea of biblical inerrancy is one of the most consistent reasons why churches keep women out of high leadership roles, particularly positions where they need to speak to the congregation. The standard reading of the Bible in these churches posits that women should remain silent in church and cannot lead a congregation in a religious service. It is possible that some women like this kind of theology and the values that come with it, but it is also likely that quite a few women would prefer an option where men and women were seen as equal in their potential for religious development and authority. The Bible, like any ancient religious text, can be interpreted in many different ways and there is no absolute barrier against reading the text in favor of female leadership. So the question remains why such options are not growing and capturing a significant chunk of the religious market.

To explain this we must realize that the status of women in their congregations is closely associated with their status in life outside church, such as in professional life and in the family. Those who have power and status in a religious group are also able to influence and reproduce ideologies and norms that favor themselves in other fields.[3] To take a banal example, a man who preaches in church may insist that men are the natural heads of families and need supportive and submissive wives. When he gets home he can enjoy his high status and feel secure that it rests on a solid theological foundation. If he were to break out of the church and establish a sect that had a radically different theology and set of values, say if he created an organization that insisted on gender equality at all levels of congregational leadership, he might attract women to his new group, but he would undermine his own position in non-religious spheres at the same time. The religious world and its hierarchies are connected to other sectors.

Buddhist state monopoly and market failure

In states like Thailand, Sri Lanka, Burma and Cambodia, which make up the world of Theravada Buddhism, the relationship of Buddhism to the political order has the characteristics of religious monopoly or oligopoly. The relative size of the Buddhist population varies between these countries and they all have pressing challenges in their handling of religious minorities. In Thailand, there is a fascinating debate going on about the ordination of Buddhist nuns. From the earliest period of Buddhism, in the fourth and third centuries BC, nuns were an important part of the religion. When Buddhism traveled out of India to new societies in Asia, orders of monks and nuns were established. There were thriving communities of nuns for several centuries in the Theravada Buddhist societies of Asia, but at some point in history the order of nuns disappeared. Buddhism had many ups and downs, and at times the order of monks disappeared too. However, it was always possible to re-establish the order of monks by traveling to other Theravada Buddhist countries and having the local community of monks ordain young men according to the rules. So Sri Lankans traveled to Thailand, or Siam as it was called, in 1753 and re-established the Sri Lankan Buddhist order, which had died out in Sri Lanka by then. The problem for the women was that the order of nuns died out in all the Theravada Buddhist countries and it could not be re-established in this way. The monastic rules (called *vinaya* in the Pali language) say that for a nun to be properly ordained she needs both a group of at least five monks and a group of at least five nuns. A woman must be ordained by a dual Sangha: both monks and nuns. When there is no recognized order of nuns in any Theravada Buddhist society, there is no way to ordain women.

In Thailand, women who work to re-establish the order of nuns have chosen one of two strategies. The first is to go abroad to be ordained. In Mahayana Buddhist countries like

Korea and Taiwan the order of nuns is still strong and they are more than willing to help Thai women train and ordain to become Buddhist nuns. Secondly, they can insist that the dual Sangha is unnecessary and an order of monks is sufficient to ordain nuns. The Buddhist authorities in Thailand have worked hard to make both of these options difficult. If Thai women are ordained by Korean monks and nuns, the Thai Buddhist monks cannot deny that the women are proper nuns, but they can insist that they are not Theravada Buddhist nuns and should not dress and behave as if they were. Their status in Thailand is ambiguous. The Mahayana Buddhism that dominates in Korea, Taiwan and China has a set of monastic rules that is different from the one used in Theravada Buddhist societies, and the religious culture of Mahayana societies is different from that of Theravada countries. It is not uncommon to hear Thai Buddhists claim that their form of Buddhism is diluted by the import of Mahayana Buddhism.

The Buddhist establishment has rejected the second strategy, too. The women activists point to the fact that the early Buddhist order—which consisted only of monks—ordained women and established the order of nuns without the dual Sangha. This should serve as precedent for the legitimacy of ordaining women with only the order of monks present when this is necessary, they say, but this argument is dismissed by the authorities. The representatives of Thai Buddhism insist instead that women have a satisfactory solution in the institution of Mae Chii. The Mae Chii are communities of women who live more or less like nuns, but lack the privileges enjoyed by real nuns and monks. Many women in Thailand want to become nuns, but are denied this privilege and instead live as religious renouncers with low and ambiguous status.

There is a clear demand for religion among Thai women and this demand is not met by the monopoly supplier. If there were a functioning market for religion in Thailand, we might expect that sects would be established that would challenge the monopoly and offer women the opportunity to become nuns with the status and privileges that follow. This has in fact happened. In 1998, the renegade monk Samana Phothirak ordained women as nuns. He was sent to prison for this.

The legitimacy of ordination into the Buddhist order has always been an important issue in Thailand and in all Buddhist societies. In pre-modern times, the Thai kings had a close relationship to the order, and Buddhism was the state religion. The king and his bureaucracy formulated rules and standards for the order of monks and the monarch was responsible for disrobing monks who did not satisfy the requirements. However, this did not mean that a Buddhist king exercised complete control over every community of monks throughout the kingdom. The power of the state simply did not have the same reach as it does in modern times. In regions where royal authority was weak, or when the realm of one king met that of another, communities of monks would have great autonomy.

As Thailand entered the modern age at the end of the nineteenth and the start of the twentieth century, the relationship between state and religion changed dramatically. Throughout the nineteenth century, the Thai kings worked to standardize Buddhist education and texts and to centralize Buddhist institutions as much as possible. The state's reach in religious and cultural matters deepened. The state adopted new technologies and modern principles of law and administration and this affected Buddhism in dramatic ways.

In 1902, King Chulalongkorn implemented the first modern Sangha Act, a law stipulating the organization of the Thai order of monks according to modern administrative principles. New laws regulating the order have since been added to this. The state church rapidly became an all-encompassing organization with the exclusive authority to validate the ordination of monks and issue official certificates of ordination. Buddhism became a tool for the king to discipline and order society, not unlike the modern state churches of northern Europe.

King Chulalongkorn's reformation of the Buddhist order was at least in part motivated by the modern ideology of nationalism. He was eager to create a national Buddhist church that would bolster feelings of unity throughout the vast kingdom, a policy that has been continued and expanded by later Thai kings and governments up to present times. In an age of nation states, the Thai authorities have seen Buddhism as the only force that can create social cohesion in a nation that contains a number of minorities with different languages or ethnicities. The central authorities have always seen missionary Buddhism as the tool of choice to integrate marginal peoples inhabiting the borderlands of the kingdom. In fact, the Thai experience is a good example of the consequences of the ideologies of civil religion, and religion as a public good, that I discussed in one of the early chapters. Few national ideologies are more explicit in the belief that the national religion is crucial in maintaining stability, moral order and community.

This belief in Buddhism as a civil religion creating national cohesion and moral order is a specifically modern reason as to why challenges to the religious authority of the Thai Buddhist state church are taken so seriously both by the authorities and by many individual monks and laypeople. But in the debate about women's ordination, the idea of civil religion is blended with far older ideas and practices that are both economic and religious at the same time. From the beginning, Buddhist monks and nuns relied on the donations and privileges from kings and other laypeople. The reason why people would donate is that donations create religious merit according to the law of karma. Religious merit works almost like money in the bank. If you have a lot of religious merit earned by gifts to the monks or nuns, you can spend this merit to secure a good rebirth for yourself, or you can even give it away to a dead family member. There has always been the idea in Buddhism that donations are only effective if the recipient is a good and pure monk or nun and it has always been the responsibility of the political authority to disrobe bad monks. In this way, the laypeople can trust that the men and women who wear robes are worthy recipients and that gifts will pay off.

In the Thai example, the tight monopolization of religion by the modern Buddhist state church is the cause of the gender market failure. On the one hand, the state church is the organization that is supposed to ensure national integration, moral order and social cohesion. On the other hand, the state church is the guarantor of the religious purity of the Buddhist monks, which is necessary for the system of religious merit to work. When Thai women want to be ordained as Theravada Buddhist nuns, they are often seen to be questioning the authority and judgment of the powerful Buddhist establishment and the laws regulating religious life in the country. A step to correct this market failure would be to loosen the state church's grip on religion so that women might ordain in the manner they choose without risking sanctions from the authorities. The problem, however, is that when a state church has a long history of guarding national integration and moral order this has consequences for the level of religious tolerance in the culture at large. Laws and institutions shape culture and values and vice versa. This is why so many of the women working to reestablish the ordination of nuns in Thailand are met with skepticism or hostility not only by the representatives of the state church but also by society in general.

What does the market perspective adopted in this book tell us about situations like these? I believe there is a good chance that negative attitudes to female ordination would abate over time if Buddhist states moved towards religious neutrality. If Thailand and Sri Lanka had free religious markets in which the state limited its involvement to ensuring that all organizations followed basic laws regulating behavior in the religious market, it would be possible to reestablish the order of nuns. If necessary, a section of the order of monks would have the freedom to break away from the larger order and start initiating women with the help of Taiwanese or Chinese nuns. In a free religious market, the monks who oppose this solution would not be able to use the sanctions of the state, the police and the courts to stop these initiatives.

LGBT religion

The Stonewall Inn, a gay bar in New York's Greenwich Village, has iconic status in the historical memory of the LGBT community in the United States. On the evening of 27 June 1969, New York police raided the place. Police raids on gay hangouts were common in American cities in the

1960s as the LGBT community were starting to become more aware of their human rights and were still often met by open discrimination from society and the public authorities. The difference this summer evening was that the people in the bar refused to bow their heads to police intimidation and fought back. The clash, which came to be known as the Stonewall riot, lasted into the night. The Stonewall riot is seen by many LGBT people as the start of a new era.

It was during this early time of gay and lesbian liberation that the Pentecostal pastor Troy Perry started the Universal Fellowship of Metropolitan Community Churches (UFMCC). Mr Perry had been a pastor for several years when he realized he could not continue to hide his real self. He went through a deep personal crisis in the early 1960s when he was defrocked by his bishop for raising the issue of his sexual identity. At the same time, his wife and children left him, an important romantic relationship with another man ended abruptly and Perry tried to commit suicide.

Perry held the first service of the church in his own home in Los Angeles with a congregation of twelve people on 6 October 1968. After a couple of months, the congregation had outgrown his house and through 1969 other gay pastors started new congregations. In March 1971, the UFMCC opened its first church building in Los Angeles and churches were established in San Francisco, Chicago, Honolulu, San Diego and other major cities. According to its own homepage, the UFMCC now has 43,000 members in close to thirty congregations in twenty-two countries across the world.

The UFMCC may well be the first religious organization in the modern world specifically established to supply religious services to LGBT people. The lesson of the UMFCC is highly instructive for an understanding of supply and demand in the market for religion. Mainline churches in the Christian world before the 1960s have mostly rejected LGBT identities as a problem or an illness. But why would LGBT people need their own churches? Many gay and lesbian people throughout history have used the services offered by mainstream churches. Why would they not be able to find sufficient religious goods and services there? It is unrealistic to expect people to leave their sexual identities at home when they go to church. If you happen to be heterosexual, it would probably feel strange to be part of a church that looked at your sexuality as deviant and bad and wanted to cure you to make sure your sex life did not send you to hell.

In other words, we can assume that there always has been latent and unmet demand for religious organizations that explicitly welcome and accept LGBT people simply because we can assume that a considerable part of human populations have these types of sexual identities. The reasons why such organizations did not develop in the Christian world until the 1960s may be found in the structures of the religious markets that have existed throughout most of history where the negative attitudes of the monopoly religion almost by necessity was the attitude of political rulers, too.

Political authorities in Christian countries have been heavily influenced by the negative attitudes to gay and lesbian people expressed by much of Christian culture and morality. If you approached the authorities in a Christian country in the early twentieth century, for instance, and said you wanted to start a church for gay people, you would not be granted the public recognition and protection that you would need to operate.

A second reason has to do with the problem of collective action. In order to mobilize and demand equal rights, one needs a certain level of self-awareness as an oppressed group. Somebody has to formulate the message in words and symbols that people can identify with and there needs to be some way of communicating the vision effectively. The 1960s was a time when several similar movements for equal rights appeared in the United States, and if we look in detail at the early histories of these movements it is clear that they reinforced each other. It is not a coincidence that the Rev. Troy Perry mentions in his autobiography that a black woman talked to him and changed his perception when he was in hospital after his attempted suicide.

These examples point to the fact that a market without any kind of government involvement is not a free market in a real sense. This is because a market where a government fails to enforce a level playing field will be subject to market failures of different kinds, as when important players in the market and other social forces try to limit the religious organizations catering to women and gay people. In a completely unregulated market, the market shares of big players can continue to grow, making it even more difficult for alternatives to establish themselves.

Free market is not anarchy

So in pursuing an argument for more freedom and less state interference, we cannot forget that government intervention has sometimes been the only mechanism powerful enough to increase freedom and equality of opportunity. For example, without state intervention racial segregation and discrimination in American education would have continued, and it is unlikely that a completely unregulated market for education—a free market in the radical sense of being insulated from all government interference—would have corrected racial biases in the long run. In the religious sector, it seems that religious organizations with closer ties to government have been earlier in ordaining women clergy than denominations not tied to the state.[4]

So should governments simply force religious organizations to open their positions of leadership to women? Is that the answer to the market failure in the religious labor market? In the Nordic countries of Sweden, Denmark and Norway there are strong state churches combined with almost utopian cultural currents of gender equality. This has made it easy for government ministries in charge of church affairs in these countries to hire female bishops and priests without paying attention to church members or others who oppose such affirmative action.

There are similar examples in the Islamic world, despite the widely held belief that gender relations in Islam are uniformly biased to the disadvantage of women. In Turkey, the Directorate of Religious Affairs employs thousands of muftis, imams, muezzins and Quran course teachers as civil servants. They carry out a number of different tasks from leading prayers and educating people to answering legal questions over the phone. Since the mid-2000s, the Directorate has very firmly and successfully worked to increase the percentage of women in these religious positions as an important element in Turkey's policies against gender discrimination, and as of 2010 around one-third of the total state-employed religious workforce was female.[5]

Governments that run a religious establishment as a branch of the state, like the Nordic countries and Turkey, have the option of simply ordering theological seminaries to open their doors to female students, and they can appoint as many women as they like in positions in the dominant religious organization because the state is the employer. But the main argument in this book is that state religion is basically unsound because the government interferences that characterize state churches have a number of negative consequences. If the state forces religious organizations to hire women in positions of leadership, it is making a dramatic intervention in the internal affairs of the group.

There is a long tradition in many cultures for religious institutions to have a certain degree of sovereignty over their internal affairs. We often think that religious organizations rest on different sources of authority from secular organizations and this is part of an argument for a natural right to internal self-government without the interference of government. In Europe, early formulations of such principles were offered by Calvinist thinkers, which is unsurprising since the Calvinists experienced serious persecution in the wake of the Reformation. For instance, the German Calvinist political philosopher Johannes Althusius (1563–1638) developed an early theory of subsidiarity, which means that decisions should be made on the most local level possible and state authorities should generally refrain from meddling in the internal affairs of religious organizations unless strictly necessary.[6] There is little doubt that this is still a valid argument as many modern states tend to forget that religious groups have a right to a high degree of sovereignty over their internal affairs.

The problem with this view is that it treats religious organizations as fundamentally different from other organizations and it elevates religious organizations to a sacrosanct status where all outside influence is frowned upon. Instead, let us try to be consistent and look at the religious market as we look at other markets. There is no reason to establish a state monopoly to create a functioning market for haircuts or flat-screen TVs, just as there is no reason to establish state churches to have free markets for religion. At the same time, it is a mistake to say that a free market is devoid of government interference. Government interference is necessary to create free markets because free markets need rules and regulations, they need independent courts to interpret laws and they need efficient institutions to implement decisions. Anarchy does not make a free market. From the point of view of government, what is the difference between a school arguing that it will not accept people of a certain race and a religious organization saying it will not consider women for positions of leadership?

Religious cartels and anti-trust

Peter L. Berger was one of the most respected twentieth-century sociologists of religion and he has been credited with laying much of the foundation for modern secularization theory. Berger wrote about what he saw as the cartelization of American Protestantism in a classic book called *The Sacred Canopy* (1969). Here he observed a strong and accelerating tendency among Protestant churches in the United States towards cooperation with other churches to gain advantage in the religious marketplace. He pointed out that a large number of denominations entered mutual agreements about how they should divide territories and populations between them in order to avoid unnecessary competition. Berger regarded these agreements as rational adaptions to a competitive environment and saw the interdenominational organizations facilitating such cooperation and coordination as an important part of modern religious life in America. So, US Protestantism quite naturally developed cartels that would restrict the number of competing firms through mergers and share the market by agreements between the remaining players. Although such mergers and agreements were an increasingly important fact as Berger was writing his famous book in the 1960s, he did not expect this to lead to something close to a monopoly. He did say, however, that "the tendency is clearly oligopolistic ..."[7] I have never seen any serious debates about the need for anti-trust legislation and action in the sphere of religion, but I do believe that it is more needed here than in many other sectors of society. Oligopoly is bad for the consumer in the religious economy as in other economies.

13

PERSECUTION

STATES, RELIGIONS AND VIOLENCE

I have witnessed terrorism only once. It was in May 1979, when I was a kid. As mentioned in the introduction, I grew up in a Communist home and we attended May Day parades with slogans about international solidarity and women's rights. That year, neo-Nazis threw a homemade bomb into the parade and during the summer they detonated several bombs in the center of Oslo. My childhood memories of neo-Nazi terrorism are vague, but when a far-right terrorist murdered seventy-seven people in Oslo and Utøya on 22 July 2011, I felt personally involved both because the victims and their families were part of social circles that I know, and because my wife, who works in a hospital in Oslo, was called in to counsel the parents and siblings of the children and adolescents who had been murdered by the terrorist. In the immediate aftermath of events like that, it is probably only natural to think about how governments might hit back and attack the ideas—sometimes the religious ideas—that seem to be the root causes of terrorism. But are ideas the right focus?

The economics of terrorism

Let us return for a minute to the discussion in one of the early chapters about the nature of religious goods and religious organizations. Many of the goods delivered by religious groups are club goods, and many are private goods, while few or none are real public goods. The misunderstanding that religion provides public goods, like social cohesion or moral order, has often been the starting point for arguments in favor of state involvement in religion.

Many of the violent religious groups that have made the headlines in recent years, like Hamas or Hezbollah, started out as organizations providing social services to members and affiliates. Sheikh Ahmed Yassin started the forerunner of Hamas in Gaza in the 1970s as he revived local networks of the Muslim Brotherhood. The Muslim Brotherhood, which was established in Egypt by Hassan al-Banna in 1928, was a revivalist movement bent on strengthening Muslim values and culture in the face of European colonialism and modernization. Through the 1970s, Yassin's organization in Gaza was devoted to charity and it was only in 1987 that Hamas was founded as a military wing. The goods provided by charitable religious organization like Hamas include law and order, education and poor relief. Members and their families would get much of what they needed in life through the organization, which would effectively create a safety net in a society where the state itself had little capacity to deliver welfare. To organizations like Hamas or Hezbollah, charitable work came first. Political and violent action came later when the organizations had taken deep roots and as the political environment created incentives for such action.

It is easy to understand why people who live in societies where the state is weak turn to charitable religious organizations for welfare services. As discussed in an earlier chapter, religious groups face a free-rider problem when they provide club goods and one way of overcoming this problem is to ask members to adopt strange or extreme behaviors and symbols. This enables a group to screen out those who are not serious in their commitment and they can also limit the opportunities for members in the wider society, thereby increasing the attraction of the opportunities offered inside the group. Religious clubs are not the only groups that use personal sacrifices to signal the commitment of members. Think of criminal gangs and the often weird and unpleasant rites recruits have to undergo in order to be accepted.

Religious clubs are generally non-violent, but in cases where political circumstances or the whims of an idiosyncratic leader make them resort to terrorism to pursue their goals, they are often exceptionally good at avoiding defections and maintaining faithfulness to the cause. They are experts at picking committed members and nurturing loyalty by offering important goods inside the group and by raising barriers against the world outside. For this reason, they seem to be more effective than other groups. By making members deliberately destroy the opportunities they have in the outside world by their behaviors, by the sacrifices they make and by the symbolic barriers they raise against society at large, these groups make their followers dependent on the club. So when ordered to take part in a violent operation, a member of a terrorist organization often realizes that both he and his family are better off if he is loyal.[1] Recruiting individuals who are committed and trustworthy is of exceptional importance to terrorist organizations and recruiters therefore develop sophisticated screening strategies to select the right recruits. For example, to an al-Qaeda recruiter previous participation in jihad is a reliable sign of trustworthiness and commitment in a potential new recruit.[2]

One policy implication of all this should be relatively simple. If a government is able to make it highly attractive for members of an extremist group to leave, the likelihood is that they will do so. The economic approach to the subject assumes that religious terrorists are generally rational and act in ways that they believe will benefit their long-term goals. Even seemingly irrational suicide missions are analyzed by economists as actions that make sense in a given context given the opportunities and information available to the terrorist. Much of the policy-oriented research on terrorism has focused on deterrence (i.e. making it costly and unpleasant for terrorists to use violence). Relatively little research has focused on the potential effectiveness of rewarding potential terrorists for not engaging in terrorism and doing something else instead. Some of this research seems to show that rewards are actually more effective than punishment in reducing terrorist incidents.[3]

If it is the case that terrorist zeal and commitment are determined by deliberate renunciation of opportunities and safety outside the religious group and, conversely, availability of club goods or public goods inside the group, as some economic research claims, this would have several consequences for how we think about terrorism. It would mean that the theology or the ideology of the group does not really matter. This sounds like a narrow position to take. I am after all a historian and philologist who became interested in economics in my thirties, and a large part of my brain tells me that the subjective motives and worldviews of individuals and groups must be taken into account when we want to explain behavior. We have to remind ourselves, however, that the emphasis on rational choice in economics does not mean that economists think worldviews are unimportant. It means they believe that behavior, including terrorism, can be explained without reference to the inner lives of those involved. Those working in the humanities, like me, need to realize that this is not a problem as long as we remember that this is one perspective among many and that economic models are not designed to capture the totality of the life world of the people we want to understand.

The relevance of all this should be clear, I think. A major challenge for many states after the military debacles in Iraq and Libya is to design policies that make it less attractive for people to join jihadist groups. At the time of writing, the greatest jihadist threat seems to be the group that calls itself Islamic State in Iraq and the Levant (ISIL). The group surprised observers by capturing large swathes of territory in Syria and Iraq in 2014 and then making fresh territorial claims in other countries, like Libya. ISIL's brutality has shocked the world. The fear in Europe has grown with terrorist attacks on civilians in central Paris in November 2015 and in Brussels in March 2016. One of the deeply worrying aspects of ISIL's operations has been its ability to attract young people from a large number of countries to join its ranks. Many states have scrambled to come up with new legislation to make it easier to punish people who join ISIL, but from the perspective of the economics of terrorism we should probably think more about the options we have for making it attractive for people to leave these kinds of movements. Seasoned fighters and terrorist leaders should obviously be punished, but if we promise years in jail or loss of citizenship to kids who made stupid choices and ended up in Syria, we are forgetting the liberal values we should protect.

There is a large literature about the relationship between democracy and terrorism and two general approaches seem to have crystallized. On one hand, democracy helps reduce the recruitment base for terror because democratic societies offer peaceful channels for political engagement and they produce fewer grievances against the political system and authorities. On the other hand, civil liberties also make us vulnerable. Democracies are open societies where governments are constrained in their pursuit of terrorists. They cannot easily restrict freedom of speech, freedom of association, freedom of movement and other basic civil liberties in order to make life difficult for potential terrorists.[4] Many have also suggested that states without real freedom of the press are better at hiding terrorist incidents to make it look as though terrorism occurs less frequently than it really does. Sensationalist press coverage is the oxygen of terrorism and there would be little point in carrying out terrorist attacks if they were not mediated to create fear among the wider public.

Religious diversity and terrorism

Civil liberties, including freedom of religion, are a significant antidote against terrorism; they constitute an essential part of the "soft power" that makes liberal democracies so attractive. States that place severe limits on civil liberties seem to be more likely to produce terrorist groups than states with extensive civil liberties.[5] Saudi Arabia is a typical case where freedom of religion is restricted and jihadist groups have found an excellent recruitment base. But we can go further and ask whether the state's involvement in the affairs of religious organizations has any bearing on the likelihood that a society will produce terrorist groups.

To answer this, let me start by reminding the reader briefly of the two opposing perspectives on the relationship between religion and state in the thinking of the two Scottish geniuses Adam Smith and David Hume. Smith's position was that the state should stay out of the religious field because a religious group with too close relations to the state would easily be tempted to abuse its position to enhance its own power. A free religious market, on the other hand, would make religious leaders behave in a moderate way out of fear of losing followers to competing sects. Hume's position was that sect leaders in a free market would instead compete by becoming ever more extreme in their religiosity, and for this reason it would have a pacifying effect on society to have an established religion funded by the state. It seems that these two different views would yield quite different approaches to the problem of religious terrorism. Is it possible to remove the conditions for such violence, or at least reduce its frequency and lethality, by following one of the two prescriptions?

Some research has suggested that competition between fundamentalist leaders, or between fundamentalist leaders and society outside, leads to a race to the top in terms of strictness. A fundamentalist leader in competition will increase the level of religious and legal observance required by the members of his sect because this will make it harder for members to quit and he will get more power and status (and perhaps money) from the members who stay with him rather than defecting to a competitor.[6] This is an argument that is completely in agreement with David Hume's view. It says that a free religious market with many small sects in competition will develop into a society with many extreme religious leaders and may also cause antagonism and violence.

But I do not think this idea is correct. Contrary to the intuitions of people who fear increasing diversity, research shows that a high degree of religious diversity is associated with less terrorism, while a low degree of fractionalization is associated with more terrorism.[7] Some research has suggested that cleavages along the lines of ethnicity and religion are associated with terrorism, but some of this research conflates ethnicity and religion.[8] Although religion may be a component of ethnicity, conflating the two in research can be unwise. Ethnic divides, especially linguistic ones, are often associated with conflict, but religious diversity in itself is not. David Stevens and Kieron O'Hara's book on religious extremism on the internet has argued convincingly that the best government policy to deal with radical ideas in cyberspace is to leave them alone and not to censor or police the internet.[9]

One of the main points in the literature about terrorism is that in the cases where religious diversity is associated with terrorism (although I have not seen hard evidence for the link) this is the result of political jockeying for a favored and profitable relationship to political power. In other words, the reason a religious group uses violence in a diverse society is the opportunity to gain something or change the status of the group for the better. This presupposes that the state is biased in favor of one or more religious group, or that there is some opening or opportunity to influence the authorities into handing out privileges or easing oppression or sanctions. In other words, we are back in the discussion about rent-seeking from a previous chapter. I would argue that when religious groups engage in terrorism, their activity can be understood as a form of rent-seeking in a society where there is a lot to gain for the religious group that wins the contest for political supremacy.

PERSECUTION

Fundamentalism as response to state interference

If we take a historical look at the origins of fundamentalism (which is not a synonym for terrorism, as many fundamentalists are peaceful) I think the view of Adam Smith seems highly plausible. In 2012, I argued that fundamentalism is a global and modern phenomenon that must first of all be understood as a reaction to a new relationship between political authorities and traditional religious elites that developed after the 1850s and in most places far later.[10] In my view, the interesting thing about fundamentalism is not theology or doctrines; these ideas vary a lot between fundamentalist groups in Christianity, Islam, Hinduism, Buddhism, Judaism and Sikhism. The defining feature of fundamentalist movements is that they are started and led by lay leaders who want to fill the vacuum left by traditional religious authorities that have been co-opted or marginalized by modern states.

The modern state came into being through a long historical process, but it was only from the mid- or late-1800s that modern bureaucracies, legal systems, educational and scientific institutions attained such pervasive influence that traditional religious elites and their specific type of authority was undermined or co-opted by states. This was particularly true of the Middle East and South Asia. In these regions, colonialism brought rapid and dramatic changes in the position of religious elites as well as a sense of a general cultural and religious crisis that had to be faced by a new elite of educated lay leaders—teachers, lawyers, doctors, writers—instead of the old religious elite that had seen the institutional basis of their authority erode almost completely by the introduction of Western models of law, education and science. These lay leaders were the early fundamentalists and they are still the most important leaders of fundamentalist groups, except perhaps in Shia Islam.

In addition to being a recent lay response to the state's undermining of religious authority, there is something uniquely modern in the globalized patterns of behavior according to which fundamentalist movements and leaders model their action. I believe that the global influence of Christian ways of performing religion has been far greater than often recognized. Fundamentalist leaders in other religious traditions mimic Christian patterns of acting when they behave like critical prophets in their own societies and preach publicly to awaken their co-religionists to action. This mimicking is sometimes quite explicit, as in the case of the Hindu fundamentalist movement called the World Hindu Council (the Vishwa Hindu Parishad in Hindi, abbreviated VHP), the leading figures of which decided they needed to structure their religious organization and action according to Christian models to be successful. If you compare the modern televangelism of Muslim, Buddhist, Hindu or Jewish fundamentalist leaders, most of whom are lay people, to the traditional standards of public preaching in those traditions, you will see that a significant shift has taken place.

In my view, then, fundamentalist movements are often reactions against the incredible intensity and reach of modern states into affairs that were traditionally the domains of religious elites. There would perhaps have been less fundamentalism in the Middle East if modern states like Egypt had not nationalized the religious endowments (*waqf*) that were the economic basis for the autonomy of the religious elite, if they had not taken control of religious institutions of education and if they had not marginalized the system of Sharia courts by introducing Western law codes and legal practices. This is not an argument for a reversal to pre-modern times where traditional religious elites and institutions had more authority and power; I am just saying that state interference in the domain of religion often has unintended consequences.

The state and religious persecution

Imagine you are a political leader in the twenty-first century with the responsibility of ensuring social stability inside the borders of your country. What will you do about religion? Throughout the world, religion has become one of the hottest topics in media debates about violence and social discord. The number and size of minority religious groups are increasing in many Western countries and some groups are becoming more self-assertive. Christian and Muslim missionary organizations are a highly visible part of public space in many modern cities, and debates about religious symbols are often fierce and emotional. Religious diversity is seen as the main challenge to social cohesion in many countries and the growth of anti-immigration movements and the success of far-right parties in Europe are just some of the reactions against the perceived threat posed by religious diversity. As a political leader you will be asked questions about how to regulate increasing religious diversity and how to manage the threat to society that some believe diversity poses.

Faced with intense scrutiny from the media, it would probably be tempting to look for ways to regulate religion to ensure peace and harmony. You could start by subsidizing those religious organizations that contribute to social cohesion, especially the long-established, traditional faiths. Perhaps you see their contribution to society as a public good. You could follow up by revamping the registration requirements, so that all religious organizations have to give a certain amount of information about their members and their religious activities. You could pass a law making missionary activity contingent on an application process where experts could deny the right to proselytize to organizations that may have a divisive or intolerant message. You could also ban groups that qualify as "cults," which means they are closed organizations that use brainwashing to convert vulnerable individuals and keep them trapped. Perhaps you should consider banning religious clothing in schools and universities just to make it clear that public space is secular and religion is a private matter.

All the suggested policy measures here sound relatively mild and they have been tried by a large number of modern states, including states in the Western world that we think of as liberal democracies. But these and other regulatory measures have the opposite effect of what they are designed to achieve. They cause intolerance and violence. The best illustration of this has been offered by Brian J. Grim and Roger Finke, two American scholars who have had important roles in developing the religious economy perspective.[11] A lot of new data has become available over the past couple of decades that can be used to compare the level of religious persecution and the extent of regulatory policies in the sphere of religion across the world. The US State Department's detailed annual report to Congress about religious freedom in most countries of the world is one important source.[12]

There is evidence that state support for religion is a cause for religious prejudice and a tendency to discriminate against immigrant religion. For example, using data from Switzerland, Marc Helbling and Richard Traunmüller show that there is a clear relationship between government support of Christianity and negative attitudes to Muslims.[13] Switzerland is a federal state with twenty-six cantons with a high degree of autonomy on matters of religious regulation and support. In cantons with a lot of positive support for Christianity, the attitudes toward Muslims are more negative than in cantons with less government support. The explanation for this is probably that people see migrants with different faiths as a threat to the long-standing privileges of the majority religion.

An interesting picture emerges, then, of the relationship between the political regulation of religion and religious persecution. Religious prejudices and persecution increase whenever governments try to restrict religious freedoms and when governments give positive support to one majority religion. Seemingly benign interventions, like government favoritism towards one or some religious groups, are associated with an increased level of religious persecution.

But what is the link between government policies and the attitudes and actions of individual citizens? Government policies are not formulated in isolation. Fortunately, very few politicians see themselves as social engineers with access to exhaustive and objective knowledge about social reality. Political leaders instead face a lot of incompatible demands and pressures from different groups and individuals, and they are human beings whose perception of the world is shaped by their own background. Most of all, they are generally quite pragmatic, which means, for instance, that if a large proportion of their electorate demands continued state support for a majority church and for religious schools, these sentiments may have an effect on political reasoning and rhetoric. In other words, there may be strong social pressures to curtail some religious freedoms for less popular cults or for immigrant religions, or to extend favoritism to a majority faith.

There is a dynamic relationship between government policies and social and cultural norms and pressures. Social and cultural pressures that are intolerant of some or all religious groups often lead to government restrictions. But this is not the only effect. Government restrictions cause religious persecution, while religious persecution may lead to more social and cultural intolerance and calls for restrictive policies. Why? There can be many reasons for this, but it seems exceedingly likely that the very reality of government restrictions gives legitimacy to intolerance. For instance, when a country like France creates laws against religious cults, or when a country like China creates laws against movements like the Falungong, this is a very clear signal to society that the restricted groups are dangerous. Intolerance seems not only acceptable, but necessary for the health of the social organism, to return to the language of civil religion that I criticized in Part 1. Policies that cause persecution can also create more social and cultural intolerance simply because the persecuted minorities fight back, either by peaceful means or with subversive and violent tactics. The result is a vicious cycle where social and cultural pressures create government policies that lead to persecution, which reinforces social and cultural intolerance and pressure.

Of 143 countries studied by Grim and Finke, 123 (86 per cent) have documented cases of religious persecution where people are physically abused or displaced from their homes because of a lack of religious freedom. The most severe levels of violence and abuse are found in South Asia and the Middle East and North Africa, but Western countries and states in East Asia also have very substantial levels of religious persecution. If we categorize states according to the majority religion, it is clear that the highest levels of intense persecution are found in Muslim majority countries, while Christian majority countries have less. It is important and interesting to ask why Muslim majority countries have a lot of religious persecution. At the same time, Grim and Finke operate with a category of countries of 'Other Majority', which means that the majority is Buddhist, Hindus, Jews or atheists. This is where we find the highest degrees of religious persecution. The authors say that this group of states is small and heterogeneous, making it difficult to draw conclusions about it. In my opinion, it would have been interesting to make the categories more nuanced than those used by Grim and Finke. The Christian majority category could have been broken down into different denominations and different levels of persecution and regulation could have been analyzed in Catholic, Protestant and Orthodox countries. More importantly, a category of Buddhist majority countries could have been used because many of these states experience very high levels of persecution. The political attempts to curb diversity are dangerous, while religious diversity itself is in fact compatible with peace and social stability.

Freedom of religion: Christian imperialism?

The Christian nations of Europe have a history of using the concept of freedom of religion for imperialistic aims. Perhaps most famous is the pressure by European powers from the sixteenth century on the Ottoman Empire to grant Christian subjects in the Ottoman lands wide privileges, which were soon used to exempt traders and missionaries from civil law. Imagine if the Muslim Ottoman ruler had been able to force France, Germany and Britain to capitulate in the same way by granting Muslim traders and missionaries immunity from the laws in Western Europe.

Today, Western governments, especially the United States, are sometimes accused of being imperialistic when they put pressure on governments in other parts of the world to make them respect human rights, and this is particularly the case with freedom of religion. In 1998, the United States passed the International Religious Freedom Act (IRFA). The State Department (i.e. the US Ministry of Foreign Affairs) established its Office of International Religious Freedom with the task of monitoring and promoting freedom of religions worldwide. The office publishes its annual "Report on International Religious Freedom," which has become one of the most trusted sources for international comparative standards of freedom of religion. IRFA also makes it possible for the United States to impose different types of punishments on the worst offenders against freedom of religion.

In other parts of the world, especially in countries with poor records on religious freedom, initiatives like IRFA are often accused of being a continuation of Western and Christian imperialism by new means. Authorities in China, Myanmar, Vietnam and several Muslim majority states have criticized the US State Department and its initiatives and reports on freedom of religion. Scholars, too, have criticized IRFA and the Office of International Religious Freedom. There are two main lines of criticism.[14]

First, some claim that the idea of religion the United States promotes abroad is closely tied to the American experience. The variety of religion that matches the conception of religious freedom in IRFA is a modern kind of Protestantism, where the individual sees his or her religious belonging as a matter of choice and where the right to convert and to shop around for better answers is important. But, according to the critics, in most parts of the world, religion does not work like that. Religion in Muslim or Buddhist or Hindu societies is so intertwined with national identities, with ethnicity, with culture, that it is almost meaningless to apply human rights legislation to this sphere. So we are back in the difficult questions about what religion really is. Secondly, some claim that IRFA is part of an imperialistic scheme to push American religion on to others. To support such a view, several critics have pointed out that the global engagement in matters of freedom of religion that was started by the Clinton administration had its roots in evangelical Christian milieus in the United States and that these groups simply want freedom of religion in other countries so that people are free to convert to evangelical Christianity.[15]

Are these criticisms valid? In the second part of this book I offered some examples from other cultures and earlier times to show that free religious markets have not only existed for Protestant churches in the modern United States. I discussed cases from the history of Islam, Hinduism and Buddhism to show that religion worked in complex ways that let many people engage in what we can reasonably call free consumption of religious goods. I specifically pointed out that there were different systems or layers of religious identities, so that members of Muslim, Hindu or Buddhist communities often had the option of choosing their own religious affiliation with local saints or devotional movements while keeping their communal or social identities ascribed by birth. I concluded from this that the critics who claim that the economic perspective is irrelevant or meaningless outside the modern West have simply not looked closely at other cultures and periods of history. A similar conclusion seems reasonable here: critics who argue that modern American conceptions of freedom of religion are incompatible with conceptions of religion in other cultures have probably not looked closely at how religion works at the grassroots level. Instead, they listen to how officials present the religious realities of their countries. These officials often have strong incentives to present things in a certain way and they often lack detailed knowledge of how religion has worked in history and how it works today outside of official religious institutions.

So I think we can safely reject the argument that religion is so different outside the modern West that freedom of religion is irrelevant. When governments in China, Eritrea, Pakistan, Myanmar or Saudi Arabia claim that Western conceptions of religious freedom are unworkable in their societies because they are alien and inappropriate, they are wrong. I think the United States and other countries should continue to press for freedom of religion in all parts of the world because bad government policies have grave consequences.

14

REIFICATION

HOW STATES FIX RELIGIONS IN SPACE AND TIME

If the academic study of religion has an important message to the general public in today's world, it is probably something like this: the things that we now call religions do not have some kind of objective existence, like species of animals. On the contrary, the entities that we today call Christianity, Islam, Buddhism, Hinduism, Judaism or Sikhism are things that have come into being through a long process that we can call reification. The word reification may sound too academic, but I think it conveys an important idea. The core of the word is the Latin word *res*, which means *thing*. Reification is the process by which we make an idea into a thing. Religions were made into things by a variety of bureaucratic and scientific practices that modern states love to do: measuring, counting, mapping, delimiting and defining. This process has had several important unintended consequences.

Religion and the United States census

The US Census Bureau had never asked questions about religions from its founding in 1790. Skepticism about collecting religious data has a long history in the United States; James Madison explicitly rejected any mention of religion in the first national census because he saw this as a breach of privacy. In the 1950s, both politicians and scholars were of the opinion that religion had now become such an important aspect of American social reality that questions about religious affiliation should be included in the 1960 census. US authorities had done some data collection about religion before this period, but not as part of the official census and only on a voluntary basis. Just after the Second World War, there was massive opposition to collecting data about religion in the United States. In light of the Holocaust it was too controversial. In the mid-50s, however, US authorities and scholars did not expect the reaction that their suggestions generated.

Jewish groups and organizations were strongly opposed to the religion question in the 1960 census for at least three reasons. First, they believed that such a question would violate the principles of the US Constitution, which clearly separates religion and government. On a more practical note, they feared that information about Jewish religious identities could be coupled with data about income and work to create fuel for deeply held stereotypes casting Jews as greedy and rich. Finally, there was a kneejerk emotional reaction of a religious community that had experienced genocide in Europe just a decade or so earlier.[1] In short, American Jews attacked the idea of putting religion in the 1960 census because they feared that the information gathered could be used in anti-minority politics and they were joined by several Christian minorities, like Christian Scientists, Mormons and Seventh-day Adventists.

The large US Catholic minority took the opposite view. Catholic churches and organizations felt that census data about religious belonging would demonstrate their growing numbers and substantial importance in American society and boost Catholic self-confidence. In the end, the skeptics won out and the director of the Census Bureau backed down and cancelled plans for a religion question. The demographers and statisticians of the Census Bureau, and the wider community of social scientists, felt that the defeat was unnecessary and regrettable. Most social scientists believe that data about religion, just like data about race or ethnicity, is in itself neutral and should be collected because it adds to the tools that science can use both to further science and to assist in policy-making. Information is in itself neutral—why not just add new questions to the census?

Much of social science research fails to take into account the extent to which social science itself creates the category it wants to measure. The counting and measuring of religious identities is an aspect of the administrative ordering of society that all modern states do. Sociologists interested in race sometimes have to defend themselves against the charge that race is a constructed category. When sociologists see race in society, they see like a state. It is a bit like putting on goggles that mimic the vision of flies—everything is fragmented into tiny squares. The sociologists' response to this criticism goes roughly like this: "Well, the category of race is constructed partly by looking at modern societies through the bureaucratic and standardizing lenses of the modern state. We do know that this modern gaze, and the category of race that comes with it, has a problematic history. But the fact is that this way of seeing and categorizing has shaped our reality and people now understand themselves in the same terms. Therefore, scholars need to take these categories at face value and apply scientific methods, like statistics, in order to understand how race shapes society today."

There is clearly some merit in this pragmatic argument and it could be applied to the category of religion as well. Religion as we understand it is a product of modern ways of seeing and categorizing societies, but as long as people actually think of themselves and their communities in these terms, scholars and bureaucrats have to use them, too. In short, then, the argument runs like this: modern bureaucracies and modern scholarship created categories like race and religion, but these categories are now so much part of reality, they have become so naturalized, that present-day bureaucracies and scholarship can take them for granted and use them as they like.

So, we end up with an empirical question. Has the modern way of seeing and categorizing religion really changed reality to the extent that these categories now appear as natural? The answer to this question depends a lot on where in the world you look. If you look at the United States or many European societies, the answer is that a great proportion of the populations in question understand religion in this way and can use the category of religion to say something about their own identities, whether they belong to a religion, or are atheists or non-religious. But we must never forget that most people do not live in the United States or in Europe, but in Asia and Africa. For the majority of people even today, the answer to the question is probably no. The category of religion, as used in modern social science and in modern statistics, has little or no relation to the everyday lives of most people in the world.

Entrenching religious identities in the Indian census

The significance of the process whereby modern states try to fix religious identities became clear to me when I was writing my doctoral thesis about how the category of religion was imported into India through new administrative practices introduced by the British colonial government. One of the sources I found particularly interesting was the decennial census that the British carried out in India and the substantial reports that were written by conscientious officials as comments on these censuses.

The British carried out many attempts at counting and measuring the populations of the various parts of their growing Indian empire from the early 1800s, but the census in 1871 was the first collection of data covering the whole of British India. The colonial government repeated the operation every tenth year, and when India became independent in 1947 the young republic continued this tradition with its first census in 1951 (its most recent was in 2011).

I cannot claim that I was terribly original when I wanted to understand the worldview and ideology underpinning this way of registering and measuring social reality. The famous book *Imagined Communities* by Benedict Anderson, a scholar of nationalism, had made similar arguments for the Philippines. Anderson pointed out that when colonial governments in Asia collected data about their colonized populations, the categories they used—say religion, race, tribe or caste—did not measure a social reality that was already there: rather, it created new social realities. The nation was one of the important categories that were imagined in this way, and it presupposed several modern techniques of registering and presenting social reality, like maps and newspapers—and the census. On this point, Anderson was perhaps not very original either. Take a look at this statement by a Muslim commentator written in a Muslim journal in Bengal in 1895:

In the last census report it has been stated that more than fifty per cent of the inhabitants of the Nuddea district are Mussalmans; but are our readers aware what form of Islamism the bulk of the Nuddea people profess? Nearly all of them have Hindu names; their manners and customs are those of the Hindus; they celebrate the pujahs; they have a caste distinction too.[2]

This writer, a local Muslim intellectual in British India, questioned the very category of Muslim as this was used by the British administration in its 1891 census. If you enumerate people as Muslim while these people have Hindu names, Hindu customs, Hindu rituals and practice caste, then what do you mean by the terms "Muslim" and "Hindu"? The article observes that when the British count Muslims and Hindus in their Indian colony, the identities of the people they are counting are unstable and the boundaries between Muslims and Hindus are far from clear.

Let us not exaggerate. It would be far-fetched to claim that Muslims and Hindus in India had absolutely no sense of belonging to different religious traditions before the British. During Mughal times, the ruling elite certainly knew they were Muslims and not Hindu. They had a holy book, the Quran, and they were oriented towards the holy places of Islam in the Middle East rather than to the Hindu geography of India mapped out by pilgrimage sites and mythology. But if we look at the common people, the poor masses, we see a different picture. To them, caste was more important than religion. Muslims and Hindus could belong to the same caste and the boundaries between them in everyday life and in ritual were flexible.

But if the categories of Muslims and Hindus were unstable and often hard to keep apart for British colonial administrators, there were other religious categories that were even more ambiguous and flexible. Just to get a glimpse into how the British administrators themselves were thinking about the categories they measured, we can take a look at a passage in the official book-length commentary on the census of 1871:

> The title of Hindoo, in the category of nationality and caste, includes many persons of Hindoo origin, who are no longer Hindoos by religion, such as Native Christians, or who have branched off from its stricter use, such as Buddhists and Jains, or whose actual religion is unknown, such as the aboriginal tribes.[3]

So, for the 1871 census, the British administrators treated the category of Hindu as including Christians, Buddhists and Jains. The British understood that their religious categories were to some extent haphazard and artificial, and that these categories did not provide anything close to a perfect description of Indian social reality. Still, the British used the census to measure and register the peoples of their vast empire, just like all Western states used censuses to map both societies inside their borders and in their overseas colonies. They classified peoples according to key characteristics, like religion, language, tribe and caste, and this way of counting and measuring served to fix identities that used to be flexible and ambiguous. In some circumstances, one could even go further and claim that it created completely new social realities.

The idea of the martial races is perhaps the best example of the use of ethnic and religious classifications in imperial politics. In the eyes of the British, some of the peoples of India were naturally more war-like than others. They had better and stronger bodies and their culture was more martial. The British wanted to enlist the martial races and build their Indian army with these people at its core. The Sikhs and Rajputs were the foremost of the martial races, the British felt, and they still dominate the officer corps of the Indian army today.

If there was anything original in my doctoral thesis, it was my exploration of how all this counting and categorization affected the self-perception of members of a religious community called the Jains. Jainism originated as a philosophical and religious system at the same time as Buddhism (i.e. around 500 BC). In contrast to Buddhism, Jainism never disappeared from India and the largest Jain communities today are in the west and south of the country. The Jains have several beliefs and practices that distinguish them as a distinct religious and social group. However, they have also shared a number of practices and customs with the Hindus, and for most Jains before the colonial period it would have been meaningless to ask whether they were Jains or Hindus. They were in fact both.

If you are a bureaucrat and you want statistics on religious demographics, or if you want to collect taxes, or dole out public funding based on membership numbers, you probably want everybody to say they either belong to this or to that religious community. If enough people tick several boxes, if they say they are both Jains and Hindus, for instance, you have an administrative challenge.

The story of the Sikhs has parallels to that of the Jains. Sikh sources from the early 1700s leave no doubt that the Sikhs had an identity as a community with their own holy persons, their own holy text and their own holy places. We can see that some of this identity was created in opposition to the Mughal state and to Brahminical culture. At the same time, Sikhs certainly shared a lot of culture with Hindus, and there is a strong argument that Sikhs were also Hindus up to the nineteenth century when the modern administrative requirements, and new ideas of what religion is, resulted in straitjacketing Sikh identity. I should add that there is some quarreling between scholars about exactly when and how Sikh identity appeared as completely severed from Hindu identity.

Fixing religions in time and space

It seems to me that the religious identities of communities like the Jains and the Sikhs became entrenched gradually between, say, 1870 and 1940, from two different angles. They can be called the synchronic and the diachronic angles. "Diachronic" points to how something has changed over time, while "synchronic" is about how something appears at one point in time. The British government, and especially the educational system, introduced a completely new way of understanding the history of religious communities. Modern British historical consciousness perceived these communities as organic entities evolving through the centuries. They wanted to find relevant sources in texts and archaeological remains to understand the origins and evolution of such communities almost in the same way that Charles Darwin had analyzed biological evolution in his book *The Origin of Species* (1859). Evolution was the great catchword of the period. From the synchronic perspective, the British administration wished to fix the boundaries between the religious communities in the present.

Both the diachronic and the synchronic mapping of religious communities had a very significant impact on how members of these communities understood themselves. From the late nineteenth and into the twentieth century, educated people from all religious communities—teachers, doctors, lawyers and bureaucrats—would follow with interest the census collected by the British and the statistics created on the basis of census data. Muslims, Jains, Sikhs and Hindus would publish journals concerned with the history of their respective communities and with their future prospects. Some of these commentators would refer to statistics that showed an increase or a decline in the size of their community relative to other communities. In some Jain magazines, for instance, community leaders would write with great alarm about the fact that the number of Jains was not increasing as fast as the number of Muslims and Hindus and they would call for specific initiatives in the community to meet the prospect of future decline and extinction. Others, like the perceptive Muslim commentator I quoted above, would deconstruct the categories used in the census, but even they would feel some concern about how to deal with the new perception of religious identity. A new way of talking and thinking about religious communities, identities and boundaries emerged.

My examples from India—and from Korea, to where we turn shortly—point to processes that in fact took place globally. They did not take place at exactly the same time or in the same way, but we can safely say that something dramatic happened to religion from 1850 onwards in all corners of the world. The way of organizing and ordering societies that is characteristic of the modern state expanded from its European core, first to the Americas, then to Asian societies and finally to Africa. Today, most states register religious groups and individuals in some way and have government ministries or departments tasked with administering religious organizations. The tools with which they carry out this task have become more efficient since the early attempts in the nineteenth century, but what they want to achieve is more or less the same. A modern state wants society to consist of individuals with affiliations and belongings that are stable and can be registered, so that administrative tasks run smoothly. The way that modern states categorize and register the religious identities of individuals has an impact on how these individuals understand their own religious identities.

The religious market in Korea

One nice thing about being a professor at a university is that I am relatively free to pursue ideas I find interesting and important, either alone or together with other scholars. As I was working on this book, I thought it would be useful to bring together some people to discuss a regional case that seems particularly relevant for an economic analysis of religion outside the Western world: South Korea. Why South Korea? It is a country that has modernized rapidly since the 1960s and is today a nation of 50 million people and one of the fifteen largest economies in the world. The religious landscape of Korean society has been transformed over the last few decades. Buddhists, Protestants and Catholics compete fiercely for hegemony and the competition has a dramatic impact on the country's religious life. I am fortunate enough to have one of the world's leading experts on Korean religion as a colleague and friend at the University of Oslo. His name is Vladimir Tikhonov. To dig into questions about the religious market in Korea, Vladimir and I secured a small grant from the Korea Foundation to invite a handful of experts on Korean religion for a small workshop in the autumn of 2014.[4] Is there a religious market, we asked? If so, how does it work?

Any account of modern South Korean religion must start with the fact that the very idea of religion has been transformed in the country over recent decades. At the start of the twentieth century, hardly anybody in Korea thought of themselves as belonging to a specific religion. Between 1910 and 1945 Korea was a Japanese colony and the colonial administration found that no more than 3 per cent of the Korean population identified with a particular religious tradition when asked in surveys. This total lack of interest in organized religious life started to change only after the Korean War, which lasted from 1950 to 1953. In 1964, the government of South Korea estimated that 12 per cent of the population identified with a religious tradition. In 1985 this number had risen to 42 per cent, and today more than 50 per cent of Koreans say they have a religious affiliation. The census taken in 2005 found that 22.8 per cent of the population call themselves Buddhists, 18.3 per cent call themselves Protestants, while 10.9 per cent say they are Catholics. These three traditions dominate the religious landscape of Korea, while several small religious groups claim around 1 per cent of the population combined.

So, in roughly half a century South Korea has changed from a country where almost nobody would say they belonged to a religion to a country where half of the population say they are Buddhists, Protestants or Catholics. Why has this happened and what does it mean? Several deep processes of social and economic transformation have contributed to or created the preconditions for the religious changes. The main heading here is "modernization." South Korea industrialized rapidly from the 1960s onwards, which transformed the country from a poor nation of peasants to Asia's third largest economy, after China and Japan, with global brands like Samsung and Hyundai. Everyday life in South Korea is saturated with high-tech gadgets; to most

Europeans or Americans, a trip to Seoul feels like a peek into the digital future. Urbanization went hand in hand with industrialization and was one of the most important factors in the transformation of Korean religion. In 1930, 4.5 per cent of Koreans lived in settlements with more than 50,000 inhabitants, whereas today around 90 per cent do so. The extremely rapid urbanization has made religious choice and competition a natural and everyday aspect of Korean cultural life. If you are dissatisfied with your local Buddhist temple, you can just cross the street and join a Protestant church. This kind of shopping around would have been far more difficult, or perhaps impossible, in the average Korean village a century ago. So if 3 per cent of Koreans in 1910–20 said they were religious, does that mean 97 per cent of the population were atheists back then? Certainly not.

"My mother was really religious, was very religious, she prayed every morning, but she would not think of herself as religious, and she would not call herself Buddhist," said Hui-Yeon Kim during the discussion in our workshop in September 2014. She wanted to illustrate the point that in the past it made no sense for lay people—men and women who were not monks or nuns—to say they were Buddhists. They would use Buddhist temples and clergy in typical Buddhist fashion, but they did not identify as Buddhists.

This is an important point for anybody who wants to understand modern religion, not only in the Buddhist world. A lot of activity that we could reasonably call "religious" took place every day in Korea during the early decades of the twentieth century. People went to Buddhist temples and prayed and donated to monks, and they paid visits to shamanist shrines to have rituals carried out by shamans. But such use of religious services was not seen by Koreans as having anything to do with specific religious identities. People did not belong to a religion. Religion was not generally organized in congregations. The exception to this was the Christian churches.

The process of reification of religion discussed in this chapter is closely linked to the origins of the academic study of religion. Towards the end of the nineteenth century, European scholars came up with the novel idea that the world consisted of a certain number of great and relatively cohesive cultural units that could be called world religions.[5] The world religions were basically shaped by their foundational texts and their advanced traditions of textual interpretation, which are the domains of learned priesthoods. Save for a few scattered tribal societies that still held on to their illiterate magical worldviews, humanity as a whole could be divided into these world religions quite neatly. This idea was perhaps most clearly formulated by Friedrich Max Müller (1823–1900), who was professor of comparative philology at the University of Oxford. Max Müller created the hugely important book series called *The Sacred Books of the East* in which many religious texts from India and China were presented to the Western public in English translation. He was also among the key figures behind the creation of a new world of academic Orientalist congresses and journals aimed at understanding the cultures of the world east of the Bosporus.

Is reification of religion dangerous?

I turn now to a far more basic and problematic issues concerning the modern practice of registering people according to religious identities—issues that are hardly ever addressed by economists or social scientists. Policies and regulation often have unintended consequences. Even simple regulatory measures, like the requirement to register religious organizations, are sometimes problematic. Nine out of ten states in the world require religious organizations to register with the authorities. The way this requirement is practiced varies widely, but in more than half of the states investigated by Grim and Finke registration requirements result in discrimination against some groups and in four out of ten countries registration causes severe discrimination.

We can illustrate the fundamental problems with official registration by going straight to the most sinister case that history has to offer. The Nazi state that developed after Hitler came to power in 1933 was obsessed with registering and classifying the German population. The Nazis believed that the creation of solid population statistics would provide a scientific basis for their work to save and purify the German race. Leading German statisticians became highly valued employees of the core Nazi leadership. When Germany invaded other European countries during the Second World War, they brought with them their vision of administratively transparent societies where unwanted persons could be weeded out.

Local statisticians became important for Germany's success in the administration of occupied territories. When the Netherlands was occupied in 1940, for instance, it already had a modern system of population statistics built up over more than a century. Its first census was taken in 1829 and by the time of the census in 1930 it had developed a detailed personal card system where all inhabitants were registered according to a number of characteristics, including religion, disabilities and occupation. This personal card system proved invaluable for the Germans, and Dutch statisticians were eager to build on this existing knowledge and create a central registry of the country's Jews from 1941.[6]

The statisticians and bureaucrats who created such lists were often driven more by professional zeal than Nazi ideology—they simply liked showing how good they were at creating population registers, just like many important German statisticians and scientists. The fruit of their hard work became essential for both efficient German administration of the Netherlands and of the deportation and killing of Dutch Jews; the Netherlands had the highest Jewish death toll of any Nazi-occupied country in Western Europe. Naturally, attacks on the archives where population data were stored became a key element in the resistance against German occupation in the Netherlands as in many other countries.

Should we not say something nice about statistics, too? After all, statistics uncover inequalities in income and status between groups. Sometimes such inequalities are the results of systematic discrimination and information can be used to do something about it. This is the idea behind the support for the collection of racial data in the United States that we find in American sociology. In India, very large government-appointed surveys have demonstrated that Muslims are underprivileged in many ways. The most important of these reports in recent years was the 2006 Sachar Committee Report.[7] Such detailed knowledge may be the starting point for policies aiming to reduce inequalities whether they are the results of outright discrimination or not. There are a couple of significant differences between race and religion as categories. Race is often associated with highly visible biological traits like skin color or facial features. For this reason it is easier to know somebody's race than their religion. Despite the fact that some religions, like Judaism and Sikhism, are sometimes talked about as broader ethnic categories than simply religions, a person's religion is mostly invisible except for outward signals like dress, headwear or whatever. At the same time, there is a growing body of literature that argues that religion, especially Islam, is being racialized in the modern world, partly as a consequence of the debates about terrorism.

Nobody in their right mind would claim that statistics in themselves cause genocide. But to get this right we need to keep causes apart from preconditions. Statistics on ethnic and religious identity have in many cases served as a precondition for attacks on minority groups, like Jews or Gypsies in Nazi-ruled Europe, or against Tutsis in Rwanda. Concepts like cause and necessary condition are not always straightforward to disentangle in attempts to explain historical cases of human rights abuses. It would seem obvious that the ideology of anti-Semitism was a main cause of the persecution of Jews in Nazi Germany and occupied lands. After all, in order to carry out genocide one needs a strong desire to do so and that desire is provided by ideology, but historians can tell us that Germany was not the country with the strongest currents of anti-Semitism before 1933.[8] If we want to see this ideology as the only or even the main cause of the Holocaust, then things don't add up. Instead, we need to understand a complex interaction of ideology with the bureaucratic opportunism and scientific zeal that made thousands of German scientists, including demographers and statisticians, seize the opportunity to make their expertise relevant for policy. In Nazi Germany and in several of the occupied countries it was the scientific elites, including the directors of the national statistical agencies, who were crucial in transforming population registration systems into tools for genocide.

I don't buy the argument that numbers and statistics in themselves are harmless and that it all comes down to what we do with them. It is a bit like hearing the American gun lobby claim that guns are harmless and only the person holding it is dangerous. I think the cases presented here add up to an argument against gathering many types of data about religious identities. If it is the case that population registers have often served as preconditions for religious persecution, it follows that a radical way to remove conditions for religious violence would be for states to stop registering people's religious affiliations.

15

IMITATION

WHY DO ATHEISTS AND BUDDHISTS BEHAVE LIKE CHRISTIANS?

When my oldest son was fifteen he underwent a newly invented confirmation ritual. Initially, I took him to our local Lutheran church in Oslo. The priest explained to us what the requirements were. Every Tuesday the kids would meet and learn about Christian teachings and ethics, and they were required to take part in a weekend trip. After a couple of meetings, my son realized that many of his friends from school went to a different confirmation class organized by a very successful atheist organization called the Human-Ethical Association. He started wavering. He considered the pros and cons and made calculations concerning the expected total value of the gifts he would receive if he swapped from a Christian to a secular humanist confirmation.

In Protestant Europe, many children see confirmation as an opportunity to get money and expensive gadgets, whereas their parents and local communities see it as a rite of passage that will socialize youth into the adult world. Religion is not a huge part of the motivation behind kids' decision to go through with the traditional Protestant confirmation.[1] My son's problem was that his family on the mother's side is conservative Christian, while many members of the family on his father's side are Marxists and devout atheists. He could reasonably expect the gifts from the mother's branch of the family to dry up if he chose an atheist confirmation. This became a real headache.

Markets for confirmation rituals

The rite of confirmation has a long history in Christianity and its theological interpretation has varied widely over time and between different Christian churches. Confirmation and the religious training that preceded it was an important part of religious life in the national Protestant churches that were established in northern Europe during and after the Reformation, but it was the Pietist movement, which swept across the Protestant world in the eighteenth century with its focus on individual religiosity, that made confirmation into an essential period in the life-cycle of young Protestants in the German-speaking lands and the Nordic countries. Well into the twentieth century, more than 90 per cent of the Protestant populations in Germany, Switzerland, Sweden, Austria, Denmark, Finland and Norway would undergo the preparatory training and the ritual of confirmation when they were fourteen to fifteen years old.

Then something started to happen. Small groups of freethinkers and atheists started to question the dominant position of the Protestant confirmation ritual, and the period of religious education that precedes it, and asked themselves if they could construct similar rituals for youth that would perform the same function without the Christian content. With the right to freedom of religion and expression taking root in the nineteenth century, it was now possible to talk about this without risking punishment. The secular confirmations started in Germany in the mid-nineteenth century before spreading to neighboring Denmark, Sweden and Norway where the labor movement in the early twentieth century happily adopted the celebration of transition to adulthood as an alternative to the Christian ritual. The popularity of secular confirmation has changed over time, but today alternatives to the traditional Protestant confirmation have captured a significant chunk of what seems to be an emerging market for rites of passage, or life-cycle rituals, in several northern European countries.

These rites of passage, and all the educational, ritual and pastoral services they involve, constitute a religious good that is exchanged between easily identifiable parties: churches and staff are suppliers, while youth and their families are consumers. Moreover, the cost of production for the supplier and the price that the consumer has to pay for the good are relatively easy to pin down. By any normal definition, then, we are in fact looking at markets for confirmation in these countries. These emerging markets for secular confirmations, where the ancient monopoly position of the national churches is slowly eroding, are easily identified in several European cities. Let us look at two: Berlin and Oslo.

The German youth party

On a sunny September day in 2014 I met three young Germans employed by the Humanistischer Verband at a cafe in the former East Berlin. The Humanstischer Verband is a nationwide organization of people who subscribe to a non-religious or atheist worldview. One of them is Daniel Pilgrim.

He is in charge of something called the Jugendfeier, a new confirmation ritual with old roots. Another is Arik Platzek, a journalist in the magazine called *Diesseits—Das humanistische Magazin*, which can be translated as "Thisworldly—The Humanist Magazine." The third is a young woman who wanted to be anonymous. I had told them that I wanted to find out how the confirmation rituals offered by the Humanstische Verband are faring in Germany and to what extent they are now competing with the traditional Christian confirmation rituals. We spent half a day talking about the current state of affairs and they showed me around the headquarters of the Humanstische Verband Berlin, where they provided me with a huge amount of written material from magazines and flyers to textbooks used in school.

The two dominant religious groups in Germany are the Protestant Evangelical Church, which dominates in the northern parts of the country, and the Catholic Church, which is the majority religion in the south and west. In the east, in the former Communist state, the GDR, people without religion—atheists, agnostics and others—are in the majority. This is the heritage of state-sanctioned atheism from the socialist period and the religious situation in the former GDR has attracted quite a lot of attention from scholars of secularization.

Challenges to the mainstream churches in Germany can be traced back to long before the socialist period, which started with the Soviet occupation of a large chunk of Germany and ended with German reunification and the fall of the wall in 1990. The Jugendweihe was begun by freethinkers in the 1850s as a critical alternative to the ritual monopoly of the major branches of Christianity. The Jugendweihe literally means "youth-initiation" and is an alternative to the traditional confirmation rituals in the Protestant and Catholic churches, although for some people the two do not necessarily compete.[2] In Germany, the Jugendweihe is often seen as a neutral alternative to Christian confirmation. The assumption of neutrality sends a clear message that many Germans now see religion as something of an aberration from a rational standard of atheist humanism.

When the GDR was established as a socialist state in 1949, the government was eager to promote what it saw as scientific atheism and stamp out traditional religion. They were building a new type of society based on rational Marxism and scientific progress. One way of removing old-fashioned religious beliefs and customs was to establish secular alternatives that could compete with and replace religion. The Jugendweihe became a key ritual in the secular culture of East Germany, it was obligatory, and in these youth celebrations kids would display their loyalty to the socialist state. After the wall came down and the GDR was reunited with West Germany in 1990, the Jugendweihe has retained its popularity in the eastern regions as a family custom for many people. The ritual has now been emptied of its socialist meaning.[3]

The main provider of the Jugendweihe today is the Humanistische Verband Deutschlands (HVD). HVD is the most important secular humanist organization in Germany and was founded in 1993 with its headquarters in the middle of the great and rather irreligious German capital Berlin. HVD counts around 20,000 members according to its own webpages, but its activities in the market for youth ritual is highly visible because of the large parties it throws for the kids who choose secular confirmation.[4] The HVD calls these parties "Jugendfeier—die Humanistische Jugendweihe" (Youth Celebration—The Humanist Youth Initiation). The parties are held in an imposing theater building called the Friedrichstadt-Palast in the center of Berlin. The kids dress up in their best suits and dresses, and the party features loud pop music with leading German singers as well as thoughtful speeches about issues like being an adult and taking responsibility for one's life.

It is difficult to say whether the number of local organizations offering secular confirmation, or the number of young people choosing this over religious confirmation, is increasing in Germany as a whole. We lack reliable statistics. However, if we look at the situation in Berlin, the HVD provides some data about the number of youth taking part every year including numbers for several years before the establishment of HVD itself. The number of youth who have taken part in the Jugendfeier has varied between a low of eighty-one people in the startup year 1990 and 3,845 in the top year, 2002. To get a very rough idea of the relative size of these numbers we can say that there are around 24–25,000 thousand students in grade eight in the public schools of Berlin, which is the target group for the ritual. This means that 9–11 per cent of the target population in Berlin took part in the Jugendfeier in the years 2011–14.[5]

Godless Norwegians?

The Church of Norway has seen a downward trend in baptisms, confirmations and weddings over many years, and this is causing alarm in the organization. There are several reasons why a declining percentage of fourteen or fifteen year olds takes part in the traditional Protestant confirmation. One reason is that the population is becoming more diverse as a result of immigration. Another reason is that more kids do not want any coming of age rituals at all. At the same time, the monopoly status of the Church of Norway has been challenged and new suppliers have entered the market and started to attract consumers. There is now something called a holistic confirmation and something called an academic confirmation. After long deliberations and a quiet, diplomatic phone conversation with his deeply Lutheran grandmother, my son chose the academic option as a supposedly neutral alternative between Christian and atheist confirmations.

However, the largest supplier outside the Church of Norway is the Norwegian Humanist Association (NHA), which has captured a big chunk of the market for confirmation. From 2000 to 2013, between 15 and 17 per cent of all Norwegian fourteen year olds chose the confirmation offered by the NHA and there is no reason to believe that this percentage will decline in coming years. In the same period, the Church of Norway has seen a slow but steady decline in the numbers of youth opting for Protestant confirmation. The proportion is now just over 60 percentage nationally. In the capital Oslo, under 40 per cent of the youth population now takes part in the traditional Christian ritual, while around 20 per cent choose the secular product offered by the NHA.

When I was writing this book, I talked to several employees in the Church of Norway who are aware of the challenges facing the Church in attracting people to Christian rituals. Some of them say that the competition from the NHA became so evident in the late 1990s that the Church realized that they had to change the confirmation they offered. One of the most significant improvements they have made to their product was to change the time of year of the final confirmation ritual from May to September. This meant that they could place an attractive confirmation camp for the kids in the summer and keep in touch with them for several more months. Surveys show that summer camps and social weekend trips are a prime reason why young Protestants want to undergo confirmation, and the change in the timing and structure of the confirmation was an explicit and rational answer to competition from new entrants in the market.

The Church of Norway and the NHA compete every year to attract youth to choose their products. From the mid-2000s, the competition became more pronounced as both organizations were allowed to use the central population register to send out marketing material by mail to all fourteen year olds in the country. It is highly unlikely that Sony or Samsung would be able to use the population register for marketing purposes in the way that suppliers of religious goods have in the case of Norway.

The two organizations are competing for the same people, but some traits make it more or less likely that a young boy or girl will choose a Protestant or secular confirmation. Youth with a stronger religious component in their upbringing are more likely to choose a Christian confirmation and statistics show that the secular variant is less successful in the counties in the far south and west where religion traditionally has a strong grip. There are several differences between the kids who see the Protestant version as the only option and those who are favorable to a secular version.[6] For instance, the secularists are more interested in gifts and less in the content of the confirmation training—my son's approach follows a pattern, it seems.

Communist rites of passage

In the former Communist states, like the GDR or the Soviet Union, governments would actively try to replace religion by creating rituals, festivals and holidays after Christian models. They hoped that new atheist rituals would become good substitutes for religious ones, and they often succeeded. Communist rituals and doctrine created by the authorities produced an atheist church much like a state-supported religious monopoly. The Communist state invented rites of passage for all major transitions in life. Children had their birth-rituals and the dead were buried according to Communist protocol. In the "red weddings" of the Soviet Union, Communist officials donned robes and solemnly sanctified marriages in a church-like setting with candles and flowers while speaking from an altar with Communist symbols and pictures of Lenin. The Communist rites of passage mimicked those of the Orthodox Church in form even though they skipped references to God and Jesus.

Communist confirmation rituals from Estonia provide one example. This Baltic country was occupied by the USSR in the Second World War and remained part of the Soviet Union until 1991. During the 1950s, Soviet atheists in Estonia created a coming-of-age celebration that they called Summer Days of Youth. This celebration was established as a substitute for the church confirmation and it was a great success. From 1957 to 1960, the number of youth taking part in the atheist confirmation grew to around 7,000 people per year, and continued at this level for the next decade. In the same period, the number of youth taking part in the traditional church ceremony dropped from 10,000 to just over 2,000 per year.[7]

But the invention of rites of passage, the invention of pseudo-religion, also took place in Western European societies during the Cold War. In parts of northern Italy, there was a significant degree of tension in the 1970s and 80s between the Catholic Church and the Italian Communist Party (PCI). The PCI was the strongest Communist party in Western Europe and received substantial support from the Soviet Union. On the local level, the Italian Communists saw themselves in a struggle to create an alternative social world and their culture was decidedly anticlerical, while the Church often found itself at war with what it saw as the godless evil of Communism. Nevertheless, in the 1970s, in some areas of northern Italy, large numbers of people were both practicing Catholics and members of the Communist Party at the same time.[8] Most of these people sent their children to all the traditional Catholic rites. The kids were baptized, they went to catechism (the weekly instruction in church that leads up to the first Communion) and then to the confirmation ritual. Even in red strongholds like the city of Bologna the Communists had little success in breaking the Church's monopoly on rites of passage and almost nobody in the early 1970s opted for a civil wedding ceremony.

Is atheism a religion?

An important characteristic of the secular, atheist and humanist rituals that I have discussed here is that they borrow their formatting from Christian rituals. There are many other examples of how the new secular rituals that are gaining popularity in Europe borrow heavily from Christianity and this is one of the reasons why it is so important to include secular rituals when defining and analyzing markets for specific religious goods. I know atheists who adamantly claim that they are not the ones who borrow. They say that, on the contrary, the Christians have stolen all the rituals that originally belonged to heathens. This is slightly farfetched.

Christianity has dominated European religious life for centuries, and when secular organizations organize their confirmations, weddings or burials in the format of Christian rituals it is not reasonable to say that they are simply returning to something pre-Christian.

Competition between religious and atheist variants of rites of passage is not only about confirmations but also about rituals connected with childbirth, name-giving, marriage and death. In Israel, a study found that mothers picked between a wide range of different childbirth rituals just after the birth of their children and that they generally did not distinguish between religious and secular rituals.[9] If rituals of religious people and atheists are substitutes, does that make atheism a religion? We do not need to answer that question with a simple yes or no, but we do need to heed the advice of Ninian Smart. He insisted that religions must be studied as worldviews alongside secular worldviews like Communism or nationalism or organized atheism.[10]

"There's probably no God. Now stop worrying and enjoy your life." The first time I saw this huge advertisement on the iconic double-decker buses in central London I found it quite funny. This was in 2009. A few months later I went to the United States for a conference and on a bus-stop I saw an advertisement almost as big as the one on the London bus. The US ad read "Don't believe in God? Join the club."

According to the people behind these atheist ads, their point was not primarily to win over religious people to atheism, but to encourage people who are already doubtful about the existence of God to be open about their beliefs, or rather their disbeliefs. The atheist campaign on buses and bus-stands in the UK and the United States is not primarily made to gain new followers, but to make people who do not believe in God conscious of their own position. The goal of the ads is to make atheism into a well-defined option in a market of religions and beliefs. It makes a lot of sense to see organized and self-conscious atheism, as represented by secular humanist associations, for instance, as organizations or firms competing in the same market as religious organizations. The process by which atheists become conscious of their own position as a credible and well-defined option in a field where worldviews compete for followers carries a crucial lesson. Atheism is going through the same process of reification that many religious traditions are going through and have been going through since the twentieth century. It is important to create a religious market that makes it possible for these secularist organizations to function and thrive alongside religious organizations and we should not forget that in some countries atheists experience discrimination.

Hence we live in a world with competing worldviews in which a range of both religious and non-religious positions are formulated and sharpened in relation to each other and in relation to an environment where the worldviews of other people seem to impose themselves ever more strongly. The famous global proponents of atheism today—people like Richard Dawkins and Sam Harris—define their position to a large extent by attacking established worldviews, like Christianity and Islam. Many young worldviews struggling to define their place in the world have done the same in the past, including religious worldviews. In such a situation, the important question is not whether a worldview can be classified as religious or not. The issue is rather the behavior and self-perception of the organizations representing and promoting the worldview, and their relationship to consumers and their relative success in the market.

The debate about religion and atheism sharing certain traits and acting as substitutes can also be found in intellectual atheist humanist milieus. For instance, Armin Pfahl-Traughber, a professor of political science at the University of Marburg in Germany, discussed parallels between modern atheism and religion in an article in a journal called *Humanismus Aktuell*, which is published by the German Humanistischen Akademie.[11] He pointed both to structural similarities in worldviews and to a shared missionary impulse that can sometimes lead to fundamentalism and totalitarianism among atheists.

On certain big occasions, most people consume religious services. Rites of passage—like name-giving, puberty rituals, wedding ceremonies and burials—are where many of us meet religion in everyday life. A human life is framed by a certain number of life-stages, and rites of passage both symbolize and bring about a transition in the social status of the individual. There is an infinite number of different ways to live a life, but nobody can escape the basic biological clock that starts at conception and ends when we die. Between these two points in time we are born, we grow up, we go through puberty, we enter adult life, many people get married, enter partnerships or otherwise create lasting bonds. Then we grow old, contract unpleasant diseases, and in the end we die.

Some of these processes do not simply happen to us as individuals. They are important events and turning points in the life of the social group to which we belong. Not even the most anti-religious Communist societies ever managed to stamp out ritual events celebrating the birth of a child or the commemoration of a dead parent. While religious participation certainly declined in some periods, the nature of this participation also changed into other forms, with gray and black markets for illegal or semi-legal religion in all Communist societies.

A telling illustration of the basic human need for rituals and symbols about death are the services offered by atheist or humanist organizations. These organizations are skeptical of religion and offer what they call humanistic or secular alternatives to the traditional religious rites of passage. So far, confirmation has been the most successful atheist or humanist ritual in Western countries, but in more and more places they have other non-religious ceremonies too. The British Humanist Association offers non-religious ceremonies for naming, weddings and partnerships, as well as funerals and memorials, based on what the Association insists are shared human values.

Most atheist humanist rituals mimic Christian ones. In many parts of the world, Christianity's ceremonial styles are the standard against which other rituals are measured. It seems that modern atheists cannot escape Christian forms no matter how hard they work to distance themselves from the dominant religious tradition. This is not meant as a criticism. It simply points to the fact that organized atheism is part of the religious market in which both religious and non-religious organizations compete for followers and define clear boundaries between themselves and others.

Why do Korean Buddhists behave as if they were Protestant Christians?

The introduction and growth of Catholicism and Protestantism have changed the way people understand religion in Korea. Catholic priests traveled to Korea from China during the seventeenth century, but Catholics were generally seen to be a menace and sometimes persecuted and killed. Protestant missions were established only towards the end of the nineteenth century. During the Japanese occupation of 1910–45, there was a modest increase in the number of people identifying as Christian, but it was only from the 1960s that Christian growth really took off. The boom in Christianity has had wide-ranging effects. The most obvious consequence is that the number of Christians, as well as the number of churches and clergy, has grown rapidly over the last few decades.

A far more subtle consequence, however, is what I would call a conceptual or epistemic transformation, by which I mean a transformation in the way people know and experience something. For many Koreans, Protestant Christianity has become the standard for what a religion is. Christianity is the paradigmatic religion. When Koreans think of religion, the characteristics of Protestant Christianity spring to mind. Donald Baker suggests that four characteristics of Protestantism have greatly influenced Korean religious culture.[12] First, Protestants stress doctrine and faith. Traditional Korean Buddhism, or other old religious traditions, would never ask a normal layperson to believe in certain articles of faith, but to Protestants, the belief in Jesus as the son of God is necessary to be a Christian. Secondly, Protestantism is exclusivist, which means that a believer is expected to refrain from taking part in the religious life of other traditions. Thirdly, Protestantism is a religion where everybody, including laymen and laywomen, takes part in religious life and forms a congregation with much stronger social bonds than in traditional Korean religion. And finally, Protestantism has been so successful in Korea because of Protestant missionary work. Buddhism certainly has a long history of proselytizing, as I have discussed this earlier in this book, but Korean Buddhism in pre-modern times did not emphasize this kind of activity.

The conceptual transformation of religion I am pointing to here has made Protestantism into the model for all religion in South Korea. As a consequence, other religions have increasingly come to organize themselves according to the standards of Protestantism. This is true of the dominant Buddhist order, the Jogye Order, as well as of the Catholic Church in Korea and the many new religions that have appeared in the country during the twentieth century, like Won Buddhism. Such imitation is evident in the way that Buddhists print "Bibles" with essential Buddhist teachings, or in the way in which some Buddhist monks compose religious hymns and songs in a Protestant form but with Buddhist contents.

The conceptual changes can be seen in how many Buddhists are more concerned with the teachings and doctrines of their own religion than was the case in pre-modern Buddhism and in how Buddhist organizations and leaders engage in missionary work to compete with Christianity. Buddhist missionary work is often more focused on making people "realize" they are Buddhists, and making them tick the right box in the next census or survey, rather than snatching followers from Christianity. In the competitive environment of South Korean religion, and especially over the past three or four decades, it is paramount for Buddhist organizations to change the way in which people perceive and relate to Buddhism. They need adherents who form self-conscious congregations. They need Buddhists who adhere to a modern, standardized concept of religion because this is the only type of religion that is counted in the government census, and it is the only type of religion that counts. All the religious groups eagerly await the publication of official statistics and react strongly to ups and downs in the numerical strength of their own group. This is one of the ironies of modern religion in South Korea and in many other societies: governments count adherents and devise policies according to numbers, which gives incredibly strong incentives for religious leaders and organizations to streamline, standardize and imitate.

Both Buddhism and Catholicism imitate features of Protestant church organization. Protestants in Korea have developed huge churches with tens of thousands of members, and in order to maintain strong social commitment they break up their congregations into cells of ten to twelve people who live in the same neighborhood. The members of a cell typically come together once a week to study the Bible and discuss religious matters and this is an important way to keep individuals attached to the church through social networks. Both Catholics and Buddhists have borrowed this kind of organizational idea from the Protestants to build and maintain loyalty.

But if just over half of the population say they are religious, does that mean just under half of Koreans are irreligious? That depends on what we mean by "religious." Two important "religions" in Korea do not fit the idea of what religions should look like. These are Confucianism and shamanism. Confucianism exerts powerful influence in Korean culture and it is in the government census about religion, but very few people say they are Confucian if asked. Confucianism is simply not seen as a religious identity. In this respect, Confucianism in Korea is seen in a similar way to Confucianism in China—it is seldom perceived to be a religion in its country of origin, but often "becomes" a religion when it settles in other countries with migrants. Shamanism, on the other hand, is not in the census, so if you are Korean you cannot state a shamanistic identity even if you wanted to. It is very reasonable to assume that many of the Koreans who say they have no religion are influenced by Confucianism, visit shamanistic practitioners or even go to Buddhist temples, but Confucianism and shamanism simply do not fit the paradigm of what religion should look like.

Buddhism as business

A key issue in our workshop on South Korean religious markets was the increasing importance of concepts and techniques borrowed from business and imported into the management of religious organizations. This is a process that has accelerated quickly since the turn of the millennium, and more research needs to be done on this deepening marketization of Korean religion. "Follower management" is now a key concept in many important religious organizations in Korea. This concept refers to the tactics and techniques that can be employed to keep adherents satisfied and to make sure they do not switch religions. It seems that the strong emphasis on follower management started with the evangelical Protestants and spread from them to other religions in Korea.

One of the key players in this field has been Pastor Paul Yonggi Cho, the immensely successful evangelical who founded the Yoido Full Gospel Church in Seoul with a handful of followers in 1958, and which is now said to be the largest Pentecostal congregation in the world.[13] Mr Cho has now fallen out of favor because he was recently convicted of financial embezzlement, but for a long time he enjoyed a close relationship to the Korean political elite. He had an exclusive broadcasting deal with a Korean television station and his religious organization received government support. With growth from five followers in the slums of Seoul to almost a million members, a congregation like the Yoido Full Gospel Church will obviously be of interest to anybody seeking to make it big in a competitive religious market.

The successful evangelical Protestant churches have often been used as a benchmark by Buddhists for efficient follower management. All religious leaders in Korea explicitly talk about supply and demand in the market for their services, and discuss how best to provide the services their followers want and need. Satisfying the public by applying the principles of customer satisfaction and follower management is seen as a "skillful means" by the Buddhist leaders. Skillful means is a classic Buddhist idea about the pedagogical principles of the Buddha; the means are adapted to the historical circumstances.

During our workshop, Florence Galmiche talked about her ongoing research into how the leaders of the large Buddhist Pongunsa temple in the upmarket Gangnam area of Seoul are developing professional follower management.[14] In 2010, Pongunsa leaders went to a nearby Protestant church on a study tour in order to learn techniques for managing followers and approaching new believers. They were warmly welcomed by the Protestants and clearly learned an important lesson. The temple now offers a wide range of services, such as a kindergarten so that parents are free to use religious services, rooms for young people to mingle, vending machines for snacks and soft-drinks and a number of shops with Buddhist products. The temple also offers a range of educational programs to followers. To build a strong market presence, the temple has used public relations professionals. The temple leadership hired a design studio to create a logo, its own fonts, letterheads and so on. The logo can be interpreted as a Buddha, as a skyscraper or as a mountain.

The oldest, largest and most important Korean Buddhist order, the Chogye Order, had a conference in 2010 devoted to the concept of follower management, which testifies to the importance of the new focus on the religious customer. Its followers are now the "owners" of Buddhism, the monks say, and the temples need to adapt to their needs. Building a loyal and strong following is increasingly seen as crucial to strategies of growth, and management science is applied to help customers connect better with their temple. The large temples carry out market-analyses to understand the needs and desires of their members. They run surveys by phone to contact people who rarely show up in the temple and try to figure out what they can do to make their services more attractive and accessible to them.

The religious life of Korea illustrates a strong trend in modern religion in many parts of the world. Beginning in the late nineteenth and early twentieth centuries, modern governments started counting their populations with new bureaucratic zeal and modern statistical methods. More often than not, the results are used to design policies and interventions in the religious market. This has in turn caused religious groups to standardize their organizations and their work to fit into the official mold. The standardization of religious groups has caused greater awareness of religious identities and much greater concern with numerical strength. It is also associated with an intensification of competition between religious groups and the most successful congregations become models for imitation. When Buddhist and

Catholic leaders in South Korea talk about "benchmarking" to create the best possible religious product, this necessarily implies imitation of the Protestant churches that have experienced success in terms of growth and customer satisfaction. Of course, how this new concern with adherence and competition plays out is partly a function of government policies. In some states, governments keep out of the field altogether, while in other states a dominant group perceives a particular religion as an essential ingredient in its national culture. Some of the religious tensions South Korea has witnessed in recent years are consequences of the close connection of Protestant Christianity to the political elites of the country.

CONCLUSION

In this book I have presented an economic look at religion in order to better understand what is wrong with the regulation of religion in the world today. The consequences of faulty government policies in the religious sector are often severe. In Part 1, I presented the basic ideas of this approach. In Part 2, I showed that this approach can be applied to times and places outside the modern West, and in Part 3 I applied some of the basic concepts to contemporary cases to highlight some of the negative results of the wrong kinds of government intervention in the religious market.

The economic approach—or the market approach—to religion has its detractors and some of them will criticize the kinds of ideas I have presented here. Instead of pondering with an open mind how economic theory might be used to illuminate aspects of religious behavior, they brush it aside because they see it as inherently bad. In the introduction, I discussed criticism against Western initiatives for religious freedom made by a network of US academics. They insist that the market perspective on religion is theoretically flawed because it presupposes that religion is a stable category that is easily disentangled from other social facts, like politics, law or the economy. But this is a misrepresentation of the economics of religion. All scholars interested in religion recognize that the boundaries between religion and other sectors of society may be blurred—or even non-existent—according to what part of the globe and what period of history we look at. But we do not need to presuppose a specifically modern and Christian concept of religion to analyze certain aspects of religious life with economic concepts. In Part 2, I used some examples from the history of Islam, Hinduism, Buddhism and the Catholic Church to show that it is meaningful to talk about religious markets in contexts other than the Protestant West.

But the far more serious charge against the market perspective concerns its implication in an imperialist project to make the world Christian. Some of the academics rallying against the market perspective on religion claim that this theoretical approach is part of a sinister scheme to prepare the ground for Christian proselytization throughout the world. According to this view, the US State Department—and governments in other Western countries—are using religious freedom initiatives to open the world up to evangelical missionaries. The same criticism is often leveled against Christian missionaries by aggressive nationalist parties and movements in many societies across the world today. For instance, in India, China, Russia, Sri Lanka and Myanmar, to pick only a handful of countries, powerful politicians and political parties engage in critical rhetoric or even physical crackdowns on missionaries because they see them as agents of imperialism.

Similar ideas can be found among academics outside the United States. For instance, the editors of a 2013 book about religion in what they call the neoliberal age spend much of their introduction attacking what they see as an immoral approach to religion. They claim that sociologists of religion celebrate free markets and condemn monopolies, and use economic discourse to colonize the social sciences.[1] They insist that applying rational choice theory and economic perspectives to the field of religion implies a neoliberal and ethnocentric worldview.

The label "neoliberalism" has become a convenient name for everything that is nasty about globalization, consumerism, markets and governance. But the fact is that most of the books and articles published by sociologists and economists working with a market perspective are more sympathetic to religion than most of the alternative theories offered by the social sciences. This is because much of the theory about religion in sociology and anthropology can be traced back to one or several of the founding fathers of social science: Max Weber, Émile Durkheim, Karl Marx or Sigmund Freud. Except for Weber, they all despised religion.

The relationship between religion and states causes trouble, conflict and anxieties in many parts of the world. There are growing fears about the political and violent potential of religion and, at the same time, anxiety about unwarranted interference in the affairs of religious organizations. These concerns are the causes of destructive trends in the relationship between states and religions. Fears about the political and violent potential of religion are the cause of unwarranted and illiberal regulations. This book has offered several examples of such intrusions and their consequences. To this we could add that states like the United States, Russia, France and the UK see violent religious groups—the latest being the Islamic State—as threats that warrant military engagement in the Middle East with dubious legal authority and catastrophic consequences for civilians. On the other hand, in some cases anxiety about violating the autonomy of religion, the fear of trespassing on holy ground so to speak, paralyzes governments when they should interfere. I have looked at some of the market failures that characterize the religious sector in many parts of the world.

Part of a solution to these problems would be to look at religious organizations as firms that supply goods and services to consumers, or alternatively to see them as clubs that cater to the demands of paying members. If governments and societies could start to see religious organizations as firms selling products, or as clubs on a par with other secular clubs, many of the current anxieties about religion could be reduced. There is no reason for governments to restrict religious life or to impose burdens or limitations on the operations of religious organizations other than those that are imposed on secular firms or clubs. There is also no reason for them to tiptoe around religious organizations, make special laws or regulations for their benefit, and give them tax-exemptions and subsidies, or otherwise treat them as an untouchable sector.

There is nothing immoral or imperialist in the market perspective on religion, as some critics claim. This perspective on religion does not entail disrespect of religion or religious people. It does not mean reducing the value and meaning of faith. When economists analyze the housing-market by looking at supply and demand they are not saying anything about the meaning that people attach to a home. When they analyze the labor market they make no assumptions about the identities, meanings, pleasures and frustrations that people attach to their work. The market perspective brackets questions about the truth of religion, just like other academic approaches to religion.

Functioning markets are never without regulation and some degree of interference. The political goal should be to create markets for religion with the right regulations and laws and with a high degree of freedom. When the critics of the market perspective describe the economic approach as a yearning for a complete absence of regulation and a quest for individual choice unhampered by any norms or laws, they are drawing an unfair caricature. Laws and regulations should aim to make the religious sector a level playing field without monopolistic or oligopolistic tendencies, with low barriers to entry and with cultural acceptance for those who change their religious affiliation. Such an approach will make it easier to manage religion politically. It will make it easier to justify the right kinds of policies and intrusions in the religious market, thereby reducing problems like rent-seeking and tax-evasion. Most importantly, it will make it easier to see that many of the restrictions placed on religious organizations in many states today are unwarranted and have negative consequences. In short, the market perspective can clarify and strengthen arguments for freedom of religion throughout the world.

NOTES

INTRODUCTION: AN ECONOMIC TAKE ON RELIGION

1. Fox, Jonathan, "World Separation of Religion and State into the 21st Century," *Comparative Political Studies*, 39, 5 (June 2006), pp. 537–69.
2. Levitt, Steven D. and Stephen J. Dubner, *Freakonomics: A Rogue Economist Explores the Hidden Side of Everything*, New York: HarperCollins, 2005.
3. Smith, Wilfred Cantwell, *The Meaning and End of Religion*, Minneapolis: First Fortress Press, 1991, p. 50.
4. Smart, Ninian, *Worldviews: Crosscultural Explorations of Human Beliefs*, New York: Charles Scribner, 1983.
5. Their views are summed up in the book: Sullivan, Winnifred Fallers, Elizabeth Shakman Hurd, Saba Mahmood and Peter G. Danchin (eds), *The Politics of Religious Freedom*, Chicago & London: Chicago University Press, 2015.

1. SHOULD PRIESTS BE BRIBED INTO LAZINESS?

1. Vivenza, Gloria, *Adam Smith and the Classics: The Classical Heritage in Adam Smith's Thought*, Oxford: Oxford University Press, 2004. See in particular pp. 54–64.
2. Smith, Adam, *The Theory of Moral Sentiments* (1759), in D.D. Raphael and A.L. Macfie (eds), *The Glasgow Edition of the Works and Correspondence of Adam Smith*, Indianapolis: Liberty Fund, 1984. See the beginning of Chapter 3, p. 134.

3. Phillipson, Nicholas, *Adam Smith: An Enlightened Life*, London: Allen Lane, 2010, pp. 64–71.
4. Hume, David, *The History of England*, vol. 3, Chapter 29, Ind.: Liberty Classics, 1993.
5. Ibid.
6. Ibid.
7. Smith, Adam, *The Wealth of Nations Books IV–V* (1776), edited with an introduction and notes by Andrew Skinner, London: Penguin, 1999, p. 377.
8. Ibid., pp. 380–1.
9. Ibid., p. 406.
10. Ibid., p. 380.

2. BEER, HAIRCUTS AND RELIGIOUS SERVICES

1. Hungerman, Daniel M., "Rethinking the Study of Religious Markets," in Rachel M. McCleary (ed.), *The Oxford Handbook of the Economics of Religion*, Oxford: Oxford University Press, 2011, pp. 257–74.
2. For a useful collection of chapters about competition economics as used in competition law, see Buccirossi, Paolo (ed.), *Handbook of Antitrust Economics*, Cambridge, MA: MIT Press, 2008.
3. Stark, Rodney and Roger Finke, *Acts of Faith: Explaining the Human Side of Religion*, Berkeley: University of California Press, 2000, pp. 63–8.
4. Dawson, Lorne L., "Religion and the Quest of Virtual Community," in Dawson, Lorne L. and Douglas E. Cowan (eds), *Religion Online: Finding Faith on the Internet*, New York: Routledge, 2004, pp. 75–93.
5. Campbell, Heidi A., "Understanding the Relationship between Religion Online and Offline in a Networked Society," *Journal of the American Academy of Religion*, 80, 1 (2012), pp. 64–93
6. Scheifinger, Heinz, "Internet Threats to Hindu Authority: Puja-

ordering Websites and the Kalighat Temple," *Asian Journal of Social Science*, 38, 4 (2010), pp. 636–56.

7. Gibbs, Martin, Joji Mori, Michael Arnold and Tamara Kohn, "Tombstones, Uncanny Monuments and Epic Quests: Memorials in World of Warcraft," *Game Studies*, 12, 1 (2012); http://gamestudies.org/1201/articles/gibbs_martin

3. PRIESTS AND FIGHTER PILOTS

1. p. 214.
2. For a detailed overview of the theory of public goods and club goods, see Cornes, Richard and Todd Sandler, *The Theory of Externalities, Public Goods and Club Goods*, 2nd edn, Cambridge: Cambridge University Press, 1996.
3. Iannaccone, Laurence R., "Sacrifice and Stigma: Reducing Freed-riding in Cults, Communes, and Other Collectives," *Journal of Political Economy*, 100, 2 (Apr. 1992), pp. 271–91.
4. James, Russell N. and Deanna L. Sharpe, "The 'Sect Effect' in Charitable Giving: Distinctive Realities of Exclusively Religious Charitable Givers," *American Journal of Economics and Sociology*, 66, 4 (Oct. 2007), pp. 697–726.
5. Zaleski, Peter and Charles Zech, "The Optimal Size of a Religious Congregation: An Economic Theory of Clubs Analysis," *American Journal of Economics and Sociology*, 54, 4 (Oct. 1995), pp. 439–53.

4. FAITH AS SOCIAL GLUE: THE HISTORY OF A BAD IDEA

1. Bob Jones University v. United States, 461 U.S. 574 (1983), p. 591. Accessed via http://caselaw.lp.findlaw.com/ on several dates in Mar. 2015.
2. See, for example, Sullivan, Winnifred Fallers, *The Impossibility of Religious Freedom*, Princeton, NJ: Princeton University Press,

2007. This is a book about the definitional problems with religion in court.

3. Walz v. Tax Commission of City of New York, 397 U.S. 664 (1970). p. 673. Accessed via http://caselaw.lp.findlaw.com/ on several dates in Mar. 2015.

4. Ibid., p. 674.

5. Davidson, James D., "Why Churches Cannot Endorse or Oppose Political Candidates," *Review of Religious Research*, 40, 1 (Sep. 1998), pp. 16–34.

6. Data From Giving USA's "Annual Report on Philanthropy for the Year 2014", http://givingusa.org/product/giving-usa-2015-the-annual-report-on-philanthropy-for-the-year-2014-paperback-book-package/ Unfortunately, this report is not free to downoad, but its results are widely cited by mainstream media.

7. Keele, Kamron, "A Plea for the Repeal of Section 107: No More Tax-Free Mansions for Dubious 'Ministers of the Gospel,'" *Tax Lawyer*, 56, 1 (2002–3), pp. 73–100.

8. Robbins, Thomas, "Government Regulatory Powers and Church Autonomy: Deviant Groups as Test Cases," *Journal for the Scientific Study of Religion*, 24, 3 (Sep. 1985), pp. 237–52.

9. Withnall, Adam, "David Cameron: 'Jesus invented the Big Society—I'm just continuing God's work,'" *Independent*, 10 Apr. 2014; http://www.independent.co.uk/news/uk/politics/david-cameron-claims-jesus-invented-the-big-society—he-is-just-continuing-gods-work-9250449.html

10. http://www.respublica.org.uk

11. O'Casey, Elizabeth, "Cameron's Courting of Christianity: Divisive, Inappropriate, Cynical and Shallow," National Secular Society, 20 Apr. 2014; http://www.secularism.org.uk/blog/2014/04/camerons-courting-of-christianity—inappropriate-cynical-and-shallow

12. *The Social Contract*, Jean-Jacques Rousseau. Translated with an Introduction and notes by Christopher Betts. Oxford

World's Classic, Oxford: Oxford University Press, 1994, p. 166.

13. Lukes, Steven, *Émile Durkheim: His Life and Work*, New York: Harper & Row, 1972.

14. Radcliffe-Brown, A.R., *Structure and Function in Primitive Society: Essays and Addresses*, Glencoe, IL: Free Press, 1952, pp. 153–77.

15. Ibid., p. 166.

16. See, for instance, the chapters in Mittleman, Alan (ed.), *Religion as a Public Good*, Lanham, MD: Rowman & Littlefield, 2002. For a concise statement of the argument that religion provides moral order, see the article Sherlock, Richard, "Religiosity as Public Good," *Politics and the Life Sciences*, 27, 2 (Sep. 2008), pp. 2–12.

17. Jackson, Robert, "Teaching about Religions in the Public Sphere: European Policy Initiatives and the Interpretive Approach," *Numen*, 55, 2/3 (2008), pp. 151–82. This special issue of *Numen* was devoted to the topic "The Challenges of Religious Education for the History of Religions."

18. http://www.osce.org/odihr/29154

19. https://wcd.coe.int/ViewDoc.jsp?id=1386911&Site=CM

20. Gearon, Liam, "European Religious Education and European Civil Religion," *British Journal of Educational Studies*, 60, 2 (June 2012), pp. 151–69, see esp. p. 157.

21. Barnes, Philip, "The Misrepresentation of Religion in Modern British (Religious) Education," *British Journal of Educational Studies*, 54, 4 (Dec. 2006), pp. 395–411.

5. RELIGIOUS MARKETS IN ISLAM

1. Bruce, Steve, "Religion and Rational Choice: A Critique of Economic Explanations of Religious Behavior," *Sociology of Religion*, 54, 2 (Summer 1993), pp. 193–205.

2. Ibid.

3. Roy, Olivier, *Holy Ignorance: When Religion and Culture Part Ways*, London: Hurst, 2010.

4. An accessible introduction to this topic is offered by Lapidus, Ira M., "State and Religion in Islamic Societies," *Past & Present*, 151 (May 1996), pp. 3–27.

5. All these names have different spellings depending on the language used.

6. Vikør, Knut, *Sufi and Scholar on the Desert Edge: Muhammad b. Ali al-Sanusi and his Brotherhood*, London: Hurst, 1995.

7. Trimingham, J. Spencer, *The Sufi Orders in Islam*, with a foreword by John O. Voll, New York: Oxford University Press, 1998, esp. pp. 225–7. Despite being published in 1971, Trimingham's book remains a classic in Sufi studies and provides an important overview of the institutional aspects of Sufism.

8. Tamney, Joseph B., "Modernization and Religious Purification: Islam in Indonesia," *Review of Religious Research*, 22, 2 (Dec. 1980), pp. 207–18.

9. Braude, Benjamin, "Venture and Faith in the Commercial Life of the Ottoman Balkans, 1500–1650," *International History Review*, 7, 4 (Nov. 1985), pp. 519–42.

10. Özal, Korkut, "Twenty Years with Mehmed Zahid Kotku: A Personal Story," in Özdalga, Elisabeth (ed.), *Naqshbandis in Western and Central Asia*, Istanbul: Swedish Research Institute, 1999, pp. 159–83.

11. See, for instance, Öniş, Ziya, "Turgut Özal and His Economic Legacy: Turkish Neo-Liberalism in Critical Perspective," *Middle Eastern Studies*, 40, 4 (July 2004), pp. 113–34.

12. See, for instance, Ataman, Muhittin, "Özal Leadership and Restructuring of Turkish Ethnic Policy in the 1980s," *Middle Eastern Studies*, 38, 4 (Oct. 2002), pp. 123–42.

13. Walton, Jeremy F., "Confessional Pluralism and the Civil Society Effect: Liberal Mediations of Islam and Secularism in Contemporary Turkey," *American Ethnologist*, 40, 1 (2013), pp. 182–200.

14. Yavuz, Hakan M. and John L. Esposito (eds), *Turkish Islam and the Secular State: The Gülen Movement*, Syracuse, NY: Syracuse University Press, 2003.

15. This argument is made in Introvigne, Massimo, "Niches in the Islamic Religious Market and Fundamentalism: Examples from Turkey and Other Countries," *Interdisciplinary Journal of Research on Religion*, 1 (2005), pp. 1–26.

6. RELIGIOUS MARKETS IN HINDUISM

1. Green, Nile, "Oral Competition Narratives of Muslim and Hindu Saints in the Deccan," *Asian Folklore Studies*, 63, 2 (2004), pp. 221–42.

7. RELIGIOUS MARKETS IN BUDDHISM

1. Brekke, Torkel, *Religious Motivation and the Origins of Buddhism*, London: RoutledgeCurzon, 2002.

2. *Samannaphala Sutta*, Dialogues of the Buddha, translated from the Pali by T.W. Rhys Davids, Volume 1, Part 1. Oxford University Press, 1995. p. 66.

3. *The Questions of King Milinda*, trans. T.W. Rhys Davids, Sacred Books of the East, vol. XXXV (series editor Max Müller), London: Oxford University Press, 1925, p. 3.

4. Mahayana is a main doctrinal branch of Buddhism. It originated in India not long after the Buddha, but became later the dominant form of Buddhism in Tibet, China, Japan and Korea and includes Zen and Pure Land Buddhism. The other main branch is the Theravada and dominates in Sri Lanka, Burma and Thailand.

5. McCleary, Rachel and Kuijp, Leonard W.J. van der, "The Market Approach to the Rise of the Geluk School," *Journal of Asian Studies*, 69, 1 (Feb. 2010), pp. 149–80.

8. RELIGIOUS MARKETS IN MEDIEVAL CATHOLICISM

1. Ekelund, Robert B. et al., *Sacred Trust: The Medieval Church as an Economic Firm*, New York: Oxford University Press, 1996, Chapter 3, esp. pp. 46f.
2. Le Goff, Jacques, *The Birth of Purgatory*, trans. Arthur Goldhammer, Chicago: Chicago University Press, 1984.
3. Cassone, Alberto and Carla Marchese, "The Economics of Religious Indulgences," *Journal of Institutional and Theoretical Economics*, 155, 3 (Sep. 1999), pp. 429–42.
4. Le Goff, Jacques, *Your Money or Your Life: Economy and Religion in the Middle Ages*, trans. Patricia Ranum, New York: Zone Books, 1988.
5. Cole, Penny J., "Purgatory and Crusade in St. Gregory's Trental," *International History Review*, 17, 4 (Nov. 1995), pp. 713–25.

9. CROWDING OUT: WHEN GOVERNMENT KILLS INITIATIVE

1. Hill, Jonathan P. and Daniel V.A. Olson, "Market Share and Religious Competition: Do Small Market Share Congregations and Their Clergy Try Harder?" *Journal for the Scientific Study of Religion*, 48 (2009), pp. 629–49.
2. Fox, Jonathan and Ephraim Tabory, "Contemporary Evidence regarding the Impact of State Regulation of Religion on Religious Participation and Belief," *Sociology of Religion*, 69, 3 (Fall 2008), pp. 245–71.
3. Candland, Christopher, "Faith as Social Capital: Religion and Community Development in Southern Asia," *Policy Sciences*, 33 (2000), pp. 355–74.
4. Sarkissian, Ani, "Religion and Civic Engagement in Muslim Countries," *Journal for the Scientific Study of Religion*, 51, 4 (2012), pp. 607–22.
5. Traunmüller, Richard and Markus Freitag, "State Support of

Religion: Making or Breaking Faith-based Social Capital," *Comparative Politics*, 43, 3 (2011), pp. 253–69.

6. Hungerman, Daniel M., "Diversity and Crowd-Out: A Theory of Cold-Glow Giving," NBER Working Paper Series, Working Paper 13348, Cambridge, MA: National Bureau of Economic Research, 2007.

7. Research has shown that this is the case in other sectors that receive public subsidies. In particular, I have used Brooks, Arthur C., "Public Subsidies and Charitable Giving: Crowding Out, Crowding In, or Both?" *Journal of Policy Analysis and Management*, 19, 3 (2000), pp. 451–64.

10. RENT-SEEKING: RELIGIONS JOCKEYING FOR PRIVILEGE

1. "Planet Plutocrat," *Economist*, 15 Mar. 2014.

2. Grim, Brian J. and Roger Finke, "International Religion Indexes" Government Regulation, Government Favoritism, and Social Regulation of Religion," *Interdisciplinary Journal of Research on Religion*, 2, 1 (2006); http://www.religjournal.com/articles/article_view.php?id=13

3. Shas is an acronym for what would translate into English as *Sephardi Torah Guardians*.

4. Yadgar, Yaacov, "SHAS as a Struggle to Create a New Field: A Bourdieuan Perspective of an Israeli Phenomenon," *Sociology of Religion*, 64, 2 (Summer 2003), pp. 223–46.

5. Peretz, Don and Gideon Doron, "Israel's 1996 Elections: A Second Political Earthquake?" *Middle East Journal*, 50, 4 (Autumn 1996), pp. 529–46, esp. p. 538.

6. Data from CIA World Factbook: https://www.cia.gov/library/publications/the-world-factbook/geos/ce.html

7. Berkwitz, Stephen C., "Resisting the Global in Buddhist Nationalism: Venerable Soma's Discourse of Decline and Reform," *Journal of Asian Studies*, 67, 1 (Feb. 2008), pp. 73–106.

Deegalle, Mahinda, "Politics of the Jathika Hela Urumaya Monks: Buddhism and Ethnicity in Contemporary Sri Lanka," *Contemporary Buddhism*, 5, 2 (2004), pp. 83–103, and Deegalle, Mahinda, "Contested Religious Conversions in Sri Lanka," forthcoming.

8. See the homepage of the Pakistani Jamaat at http://jamaat.org/en/jamaatOrDawat.php?cat_id=11

11. MONOPOLY: NORDIC STATE CHURCHES AND COMMUNIST REPRESSION

1. Yang, Fenggang, *Religion in China: Survival and Revival under Communist Rule*, Oxford: Oxford University Press, 2012. All of what I say about the Chinese religious market here is based on this book.

2. Christiansen, Henrik, "Kirketilhørsforholdene i den danske kirke," in Palmqvist, Arne (ed.), *Att höra till folkkyrkan*, Klippan: Petra bokførlag, 1984, pp. 29–62, quote from p. 30.

3. See their homepage at https://www.liberalalliance.dk/. Unfortunately, there is no English version.

4. Lausten, Martin Schwarz, *Christian den 3. og kirken 1537–1559*, Copenhagen: Akademisk forlag, 1987, pp. 129ff. Lausten discusses the use of the term "police" at the time, which clearly had slightly wider connotations than today.

5. Brekke, Torkel, *Gud i norsk politikk*, Oslo: Pax forlag, 2002, pp. 109f.

6. Alvunger, Daniel, *Nytt Vin, Gamla Läglar. Socialdemokratisk kyrkopolitik under perioden 1944–1973*, Gothenburg: Församlingsförlaget, 2006.

7. Brekke, *Gud i norsk politikk*, p. 109.

8. Hamberg, Eva M. and Thorleif Pettersson, "The Religious Market: Denominational Competition and Religious Participation in Contemporary Sweden," *Journal for the Scientific Study of Religion*, 33, 3 (Sep. 1994), pp. 205–16.

9. This discussion of mega-churches borrows extensively from the

argumentation in the following article: Wollschleger, Jason and Jeremy R. Porter, "A 'WalMartization' of Religion? The Ecological Impact of Megachurches on the Local and Extra-Local Religious Economy," *Review of Religious Research*, 53, 3 (Dec. 2011), pp. 279–99.

12. DISCRIMINATION: WOMEN, GAY PEOPLE AND GOD

1. Stark, Rodney, "Physiology and Faith: Addressing the 'Universal' Gender Difference in Religious Commitment," *Journal for the Scientific Study of Religion*, 41, 3 (Sep. 2002), pp. 495–507.
2. Adams, Jimi, "Stained Glass Makes the Ceiling Visible: Organizational Opposition to Women in Congregational Leadership," *Gender & Society*, 21, 1 (Feb. 2007), pp. 80–105.
3. Bush, Evelyn, "Explaining Religious Market Failure: A Gendered Critique of the Religious Economies Model," *Sociological Theory*, 28, 3 (Sep. 2010), pp. 304–25.
4. Chaves, Mark, *Ordaining Women: Culture and Conflict in Religious Organizations*, Cambridge, MA: Harvard University Press, 1997, p. 43.
5. Hassan, Mona, "Women Preaching for the Secular State: Official Female Preachers (Bayan Vaizler) in Contemporary Turkey," *International Journal of Middle Eastern Studies*, 43 (2011), pp. 451–73.
6. Hueglin, Thomas, "Johannes Althusius: Medieval Constitutionalist or Modern Federalist?" *Publius*, 9, 4 (1979), pp. 9–41.
7. Berger, Peter L., *The Sacred Canopy: Elements of a Sociological Theory of Religion*, New York: Doubleday, 1969, p. 144.

13. PERSECUTION: STATES, RELIGIONS AND VIOLENCE

1. This is part of the argument in Berman, Eli, *Radical, Religious and Violent: The New Economics of Terrorism*, Cambridge, MA:

MIT Press, 2009. See also Iannaccone, Laurence R. and Eli Berman "Religious Extremism: The Good, the Bad, and the Deadly," *Public Choice*, 128, 1–2 (July 2006), pp. 109–29.

2. Hegghammer, Thomas (2012) "The recruiter's dilemma: Signaling and rebel recruitment tactics," *Journal of Peace Research*, 50(1), pp. 3–16.

3. Dugan, Laura and Erika Chenoweth (2012) "Moving Beyond Deterrence: The Effectiveness of Raising the Expected Utility of Abstaining from Terrorism in Israel," *American Sociological Review*, 77, 4 (Aug. 2012), pp. 597–624.

4. Li, Quan, "Does Democracy Promote or Reduce Transnational Terrorist Incidents?" *Journal of Conflict Resolution*, 49, 2 (Apr. 2005), pp. 278–97. This was a special issue of the *Journal of Conflict Resolution* about the political economy of terrorism; the other articles in the issue will be of interest to anybody interested in the subject matter.

5. Krueger, Alan B., *What Makes a Terrorist? Economics and the Roots of Terrorism*, Princeton, NJ: Princeton University Press, 2007, pp. 78–9, 86–9.

6. Epstein, Gil S. and Ira N. Gang, "Understanding the Development of Fundamentalism," *Public Choice*, 132, 3–4 (Sep. 2007), pp. 257–71.

7. Blomberg, S. Brock and Gregory D. Hess, "The Lexus and the Olive Branch: Globalization, Democratization, and Terrorism," in Keefer, Philip and Norman Loayza (eds), *Terrorism, Economic Development, and Political Openness*, New York: Cambridge University Press, 2008, pp. 116–48, see esp. pp. 130–2.

8. Piazza, James A., "Rooted in Poverty? Terrorism, Poor Economic Development, and Social Cleavages," *Terrorism and Political Violence*, 18, 1 (2006), pp. 159–77.

9. Stevens, David and Kieron O'Hara, *The Devil's Long Tail: Religious and Other Radicals in the Internet Marketplace*, London: Hurst, 2015.

10. Brekke, Torkel, *Fundamentalism: Prophecy and Protest in an*

Age of Globalization, New York: Cambridge University Press, 2012.

11. Grim, Brian J. and Roger Finke, *The Price of Freedom Denied: Religious Persecution and Conflict in the 21st Century*, New York: Cambridge University Press, 2011. The research for their book was partly published in journals, but here I use the book as my main source.

12. Country reports can be accessed via www.state.gov/j/drl/rls/irf/

13. Helbling, Marc and Richard Traunmüller (2014) "How State Support of Religion Shapes Attitudes toward Muslims," Social Science Research Network; http://papers.ssrn.com/sol3/papers.cfm?abstract_id=2416426

14. Fore, Matthew L. "Shall Weigh Your God and You: Assessing the Imperialistic Implications of the International Religious Freedom Act in Muslim Countries," *Duke Law Journal*, 52, 2 (Nov. 2002), pp. 423–53.

15. See, for instance, Nichols, Joel A., "Evangelicals and Human Rights: The Continuing Ambivalence of Evangelical Christians' Support for Human Rights," *Journal of Law and Religion*, 24, 2 (2008–9), pp. 629–62.

14. REIFICATION: HOW STATES FIX RELIGIONS IN SPACE AND TIME

1. Schultz, Kevin M. "Religion as Identity in Postwar America: The Last Serious Attempt to Put a Question on Religion in the United States Census," *Journal of American History*, 93, 2 (Sep. 2006), pp. 359–84.

2. Sharif in *The Moslem Chronicle*, 1895, quoted in Ahmed, Rafiuddin, *The Bengal Muslims*, Oxford: Oxford University Press, 1996, p. 7.

3. Memorandum on the Census of British India of 1871–2. London, 1875. p. 20.

4. The participants at the workshop were Vladimir Tikhonov (Oslo University), Donald Baker (University of British Columbia, Vancouver), Florence Galmiche (University of Paris-Diderot), Hwang Soonil (Dongguk University, Seoul) and Hui-Yeon Kim (INALCO, Paris), as well as myself and some graduate students working on Korean religion.

5. Masuzawa, Tomoko, *The Invention of World Religions*, Chicago: Chicago University Press, 2005.

6. Aly, Götz and Karl Heinz Roth, *The Nazi Census: Identification and Control in the Third Reich*, Philadelphia: Temple University Press, 2004, pp. 66–86.

7. It can be downloaded from the webpages of the Ministry of Minority Affairs, see http://www.minorityaffairs.gov.in/sachar

8. William I. Brustein offers interesting surveys of anti-Semitic articles in newspapers in different countries in different periods prior to the Second World War in Brustein, William I., *Roots of Hate: Anti-Semitism in Europe before the Holocaust*, Cambridge: Cambridge University Press, 2003.

15. IMITATION: WHY DO ATHEISTS AND BUDDHISTS BEHAVE LIKE CHRISTIANS?

1. Christensen, Leise et al. (2010) "Protestant Confirmation in a European Perspective," in Collins-Mayo, Sylvia and Pink Dandelion (eds), *Religion and Youth*, Farnham: Ashgate, 2010.

2. Meier, Andreas, "Struktur und Geschichte der Jugendweihen/ Jugendfeiern," Working Paper no. 8, Konrad Adenauer Stiftung, Sankt Augustin, 2001.

3. Weyel, Birgit, "Die Jugendweihe: Die Dynamik eines Rituals zwischen Beharrung und Wandel," *Berliner Theologische Zeitschrift*, 26 (2009), pp. 31–46.

4. www.humanismus.de

5. All of these data are from HVD and I would like to thank Mr Daniel Pilgrim, project leader in JugendFEIER, HVD, for his generous help.

6. Høeg, Ida Marie, "Friheten til a tenke og mene hva du vil er en menneskerett," in Krupla, Bernd and Ingrid Reite (eds), *Mellom Pietisme og Pluralitet*, Oslo: Iko, 2010, pp. 168–94.

7. Froese, Paul, *The Plot to Kill God: Findings from the Soviet Experiment in Secularization*, Berkeley: University of California Press, 2008, pp. 112f. Some of the same points were made in Froese, Paul, "Forced Secularization in Soviet Russia: Why an Atheistic Monopoly Failed," *Journal for the Scientific Study of Religion*, 43, 1 (Mar. 2004), pp. 35–50. On Estonian confirmation rituals, Froese quotes material from a book by David E. Powell, which I have not been able to consult myself.

8. See Kertzer, David I., *Comrades and Christians: Religion and Political Struggle in Communist Italy*, New York: Cambridge University Press, 1980. For a brief discussion of the ritual side of the Catholic–Communist relationship, see Kertzer, David I., "Participation of Italian Communists in Catholic Rituals: A Case Study," *Journal for the Scientific Study of Religion*, 14, 1 (Mar. 1975), pp. 1–11.

9. Sered, Susan Starr, "Religious Rituals and Secular Rituals: Interpenetrating Models of Childbirth in a Modern, Israeli Context," *Sociology of Religion*, 54, 1 (1993), pp. 101–14.

10. Smart, Ninian, *Worldviews: Crosscultural Explorations of Human Beliefs*, New York: Charles Scribner, 1983.

11. Pfahl-Traughber, Armin, "Ist der Atheismus auch eine Religion?" *Humanismus Aktuell*, 23 (2009), pp. 42–52.

12. Professor Baker's insights are borrowed from his paper given at the workshop already referred to.

13. See, for instance, Anderson, Allan, *An Introduction to Pentecostalism: Global Charismatic Christianity*, Cambridge: Cambridge University Press, 2004, p. 1.

14. Professor Galmiche's insights are borrowed from her paper given at the workshop already referred to.

CONCLUSION

1. Martikainen, Tuomas and François Gauthier (eds), *Religion in the Neoliberal Age: Political Economy and Modes of Governance*, Farnham: Ashgate, 2013, p. 7.

INDEX

Abbasid Caliphate (750–1258/1261–1517): 80
Afghanistan: 114; death-sentences for apostasy in, 170
agnosticism: 23, 244
Agudat Yisrael: merger with Degel HaTorah, 159
Ajivikism: 121
Alevis: 94, 96–7; NGOs, 97
Algeria: 80
Ali: family of, 81
Althusius, Johannes: theory of subsidiarity, 201
ancient Greece: 13
Anderson, Benedict: *Imagined Communities*, 227
apostasy: punishments for, 170–1
Arabic (language): 67
Aristotle: *Nicomachean Ethics*, 13
Arjuna (character): 100
Ashoka: role in development of Buddhism, 118–22
Atatürk, Mustafa Kemal: 92–3, 95–6; death of, 94
atheism: 2, 7, 15, 23, 219, 242–3, 250–3; confirmations, 247; humanist, 245, 253–4; organizations, 7, 27; organized, 251; reification of, 252; rituals of, 253–4
al-Azhar University: 80–1; establishment of, 80
Australia: 68; totemism in, 68
Austria: Protestant population of, 242
Avalokiteshavra: 124

Baker, Donald: observations of Korean religious culture, 255
Balkan Wars (1912–13): 92
al-Banna, Hassan: founder of Muslim Brotherhood, 206
Belgium: Brussels Bombings (2016), 209
Bellah, Robert N.: 64, 144; role in development of concept of civil religion, 62
Benedict, Saint: Rule of, 129
Berger, Peter L.: 203; *Sacred Canopy, The* (1969), 202
bhakti movement: 101–3, 138, 140
Blond, Phillip: 64; influence over Big Society concept, 63
Bob Jones University: revoking of tax exempt status of (1983), 57

285

INDEX

Bon: 123–4

Breivik, Anders: perpetrator of Utoya Massacre (2011), 205

British Humanist Association: 254

Bruce, Steve: 77; criticism of studies of local religious markets, 183

Buddha Amitabha: 124

Buddhism: 1, 46, 78, 87, 115–16, 137, 147, 167, 174, 187–8, 191, 193–4, 219, 221, 223, 229, 234–5, 256–7, 259–61, 264; as civil religion, 194–5; Chogye Order, 260; conception of salvation, 101; development of, 101, 118–23, 194; Dhammayut, 127; fundamentalist, 213; Geluk, 124–5; influence on religious activity in online gaming, 36; karma, 116–17, 161, 172, 195; Mae Chii, 192; Maha Nikya, 127; Mahayana, 123–4, 191–2; missionary organizations, 8, 256; Pali, 111, 126, 191; Pongunsa, 259; religious markets of, 120–1; *Questions of King Milinda, The*, 114–15; religious identities of, 138; Sangha, 119–20, 126–7, 191–2, 194; *suttas*, 111–14; Theravada, 111, 126, 190–1, 195; Tibetan, 123–4

Burger, Chief Justice Warren: 58

Burma: Theravada Buddhism in, 111, 171, 190–1

Calvinism: 201

Cambodia: Theravada Buddhism in, 111, 190–1

Cameron, David: concept of Big Society, 63; religious rhetoric of, 63–4

capitalism: 13, 137, 173, 180; crony, 155–6

Cantwell Smith, Wilfred: 7

Carl V, Emperor: 177

Catholic Church/Catholicism: 22–3, 44, 89, 106, 129, 131, 136, 161, 174, 184–7, 219, 244, 250, 254, 257, 261, 264; catechism, 250; conception of salvation, 136–7; indulgences, 136; Mass, 6; missionaries, 254–5; monasteries, 131, 134; opposition to census data collection by followers of, 224–5; purgatory, 137; religious goods of, 132–3; religious identity of, 138; rites of passage, 250

China, Imperial (221BC–1911AD): Catholic/Protestant missionary efforts in 254–5

China, People's Republic of: 5, 24, 222, 264; Cultural Revolution (1966–76), 174; economy of, 234; Hong Kong, 155; influence of Confucianism in, 257–8; Mahayana Buddhism in, 191–2; repression of religion in, 174, 218

Chishti (Sufi *tariqa*): 83

286

INDEX